COMPARATIVE POLITICS OF NORTH AFRICA

Contemporary Issues in the Middle East

COMPARATIVE POLITICS
OF NORTH AFRICA

Algeria, Morocco, and Tunisia

John P. Entelis

SYRACUSE UNIVERSITY PRESS

1980

Library of Congress Cataloging in Publication Data
Entelis, John Pierre, 1941–
    Comparative politics of North Africa.
    (Contemporary issues in the Middle East)
    Bibliography: p.
    Includes index.
    1.   Africa, North—Politics and government.

I.   Title.   II.   Series: Contemporary issues in the
Middle East series.
JQ3189.A2E57   320.3′096   80-10155
ISBN 0-8156-2214-7

à Françoise, Dominique, et Joëlle —
Lovingly

JOHN P. ENTELIS was Senior Fulbright Professor at the Institut des Sciences Politiques et de l'Information of the University of Algiers, 1977–78. He is currently Professor of Political Science and Director of the Graduate Program in International Political Economy and Development at Fordham University and author of *Arab Oil* and *Pluralism and Party Transformation in Lebanon.*

CONTENTS

TABLES

PREFACE

THIS SURVEY constitutes an introductory level comparison of the contemporary political systems of North Africa or, as known in Arabic, the Maghrib—Algeria, Morocco, and Tunisia. It is intended for nonspecialists and undergraduate students interested in the history and politics of the Middle East and North Africa. It can also be used as a supplementary text in courses dealing with general African politics, comparative political development, the politics of the developing areas, and political development and social change in the Third World.

Between the encyclopedic reference work of W. Knapp, *North West Africa*, and the few excellent yet highly specialized comparative political studies—all dated and out-of-print save one—there has not been an English-language introduction to the politics of North Africa available for nearly a decade. This text is intended to fill this obvious void on a subject that is increasingly capturing public and professional attention but which for too long has been the exclusive domain of French-language scholars or American specialists writing at levels and in a language far removed from the experiences and backgrounds of most beginning students of the subject.

After providing an historical overview and demographic profile of the area along with an analysis of the differing modes and consequences of European colonial penetration, the book systematically discusses each political system according to common categories of analysis thereby making comparison useful and interesting: postindependence politics, political culture and ideology, political structures, political processes, political economy, and foreign policy. The book includes a bibliography of English-language book titles that beginning students will find useful as a guide to further reading.

Part of the research in Algeria and Morocco was undertaken while the author was Senior Fulbright Professor at the Institute des Sciences Politiques et de l'Information of the University of Algiers in 1977–78. Earlier work in Tunisia and France was funded by generous grants from Fordham University's Research Council and its Office of Research Services along with a Faculty Research Grant from the Joint Committee on the Near and Middle East of the Social Science Research Council and the American Council of Learned Societies. None of the above institutions or granting agencies are responsible for the ideas here presented which are solely those of the author.

This book is dedicated to the three lovely females in my life who shared in the discovery, adventure, (and misadventure) that made living and traveling in the Maghrib such a memorable experience.

River Edge, New Jersey   John P. Entelis
November 1979

COMPARATIVE POLITICS OF NORTH AFRICA

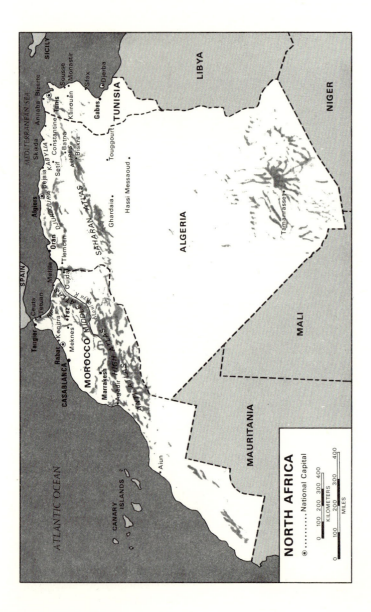

NORTH AFRICA
⊛ ········ National Capital

KILOMETERS
0 100 200 300 400

MILES
0   100   200   300   400

INTRODUCTION

NORTH AFRICA constitutes a distinctive and unique world of its own, however much it may share in culture, religion, language, and history with the Arab Middle East. Unlike the Middle East, the history of North Africa has been marked by great cultural unity and a high degree of ethnic and religious homogeneity. Even today, despite the existence of three separate, independent political entities, the similarities of the whole eclipse the divergence of its parts.

THE LAND

The distinctiveness of the region is in great part a function of its geographical features. It was the nomadic Arab invaders in the seventh century A.D. who gave the area the name *jazirat al-maghrib* ("island of the west"), a virtually self-contained region bounded by the Mediterranean Sea on the north, the Atlantic Ocean on the west, the great Sahara in the south, and by three hundred miles of desert running to the Mediterranean between Tripolitania and Cyrenaica in the east. The term North Africa or *Afrique du Nord* came into being during the 130 years of European colonial rule and today is used by the peoples of the Maghrib themselves in referring to the three countries of Morocco, Algeria, and Tunisia. The Maghrib today refers to the "western" Arab world as opposed to the "eastern" or Mashriq Arab world of the Middle East.

Although the transition from the vegetation of the Mediterranean to the barren desolateness of the desert is nowhere exactly the same, in general the following north-south patterns tend to reduplicate themselves in the area known as "useful North Africa" or the "open Maghrib," that is, the geographical quadrilateral formed by drawing an imaginary line just below Agadir in southwest Morocco to the Mediterranean shore at 12° E longitude: coastal valleys and plains, followed by mountains, high steppes, more mountains, and finally desert. The most noteworthy geographical element is the long and basically continuous chain of mountains, the Atlas, which forms a horizontal backbone running across the entire length of the three countries from southwest Morocco to northeast Tunisia. Filled with steep valleys and narrow gorges, this unbroken mountain chain, successfully cutting off the desert to the south from the more fertile areas north of it, has denied permanent occupation and control to all invaders.

Reinforcing the island quality of the Maghrib is the virtual absence of navigable rivers. In all of the three countries, only the Sebu River, originating in the Atlas and flowing to Kenitra in Morocco, can be called a transportation aid. The Mediterranean coastal entries thus constitute the sole link to waterways. There are few good natural harbors, however. Casablanca and Algiers have been developed and are the sole exceptions.

The climate of the coastal plain is essentially Mediterranean, with warm, dry summers, hotter in the east than in the west, where the cool Canaries current reduces temperatures along Moroccan shores, and mild, rainy winters. Inland temperatures go up rapidly in the summer and down in winter.

Rainfall varies greatly in the Maghrib, determined, in

large part, by the location of the mountains and the prevailing winds. Rainfall is concentrated in a few winter months and where it is plentiful tends to fall in areas in which the land is either too high or too rugged for effective cultivation. The area shows in its climate the same extremes exhibited elsewhere, ranging from a maritime to a continental climate, and with rainfall ranging from seventy or more inches in parts of Algeria to less than four inches in the Tozeur area of southwest Tunisia.

THE PEOPLE

The original inhabitants of North Africa are the Berbers, six million or so of whom today are found predominantly in Morocco and Algeria and whose principal distinguishing characteristic is their individualistic language, Berberophone. This is an exclusively colloquial language which is still used in the home, the fields, and by the women. Arabized Berbers speak dialectical Arabic in their associations with outsiders, in the world of commerce, and it is the language of the men.

Large groups of Berbers are found in the Kabyle and Aurès mountains of Algeria, while the largest concentrations of Berberophone-speaking people are found principally in the central and southern Atlas of Morocco, with smaller but significant concentrations also found in the Rif. The percentages of the total populations which speak Berberophone in Algeria and Morocco are estimated as high as 25 and 40 percent, respectively. Tunisia, because of its historic geographical accessibility, is today virtually devoid of any non-Arabic-speaking Berbers.

The key to understanding Berber-Arab relations is that although both possess distinct languages, histories, and customs, these do not constitute categories of separation or conflictual cleavages. For all practical purposes contemporary Berbers have been thoroughly "Islamicized" and "Arabized" as it pertains to the question of religious and cultural identity. Unlike the Kurds in Iraq, Iran, and Turkey or the Christian Copts in Egypt, the Berbers have not developed a nationalist movement of their own to challenge the legitimacy of Arab nationalist aspirations, nor did Christianity among the Berbers survive as it did in Egypt.

In sum, while some Berbers are clearly identifiable (for example, the Kabyle in Algeria), for the most part the difference between Arabized Berbers, or Arabs living in Berber areas, is neither very obvious nor of political or practical significance. It would be a mistake therefore, to overly dramatize the cultural distinctions between Berbers and Arabs.

Aside from the original Berber inhabitants and Arabized Berbers, the most important contribution to the population of the Maghrib has been made by the Arabs. The Arabs arrived in North Africa in the mid-seventh century and over a period of several hundred years managed to transform the Berber-populated Maghrib into an integral part of the Arabo-Islamic world. In terms of culture, language, and religion, the Arabs profoundly and permanently affected North African society.

A third group that has made significant contributions to and helped shape the human scene in North Africa has been the Europeans. Its oddity, however, lies in the fact that it has not in any way altered the racial composition of the indigenous people. In fact, it may safely be stated that, like the Romans and the Vandals of the past, the Europeans of today will leave no ethnic imprint on the Maghrib. When the Europeans arrived in significant numbers in the 1830s, they established an alien life bringing with them their own social, economic, and cultural patterns. Throughout their stay in North Africa, they remained remarkably unaffected by their environment and all other inhabitants of the area. Yet despite their relatively brief presence in the Maghrib and their virtual isolation from native society, the Europeans induced profound and, in some cases, irreversible changes in that society. Among other much smaller groups that inhabited or continue to inhabit North Africa are Spanish Muslims, the Jews, the Turks, and the Negroes. With political independence, the mass exodus of Europeans, the creation of the state of Israel, and the long-term process of Arabization and Islamization, the Maghrib of today is ethnically, culturally, and religiously homogeneous. Virtually all significant numbers of Europeans (French, Spanish, and Italian), indigenous Jews, and other indigenous and nonindigenous non-Muslim Arabs have departed from North Africa. Probably the most ethnically fragmented and socially pluralistic North African state, Morocco, is gradually becoming unified with only the Spanish enclaves of Ceuta and Melilla remaining undisturbed. At the time of independence in 1956, Tangier lost its international status and reverted back to Moroccan sovereignty. In 1969, the Spanish enclave of Ifni on the Atlantic coast was incorporated into Morocco. Finally, in 1976, former Spanish Sahara was divided between Morocco, obtaining the northern two-thirds, and Mauritania, which annexed the southern third. This decision was met immediately by the organized resistance of the so-called Polisario Front seeking separate independence for the Sahara and militarily and politically supported by Algeria. When Mauritania signed a separate peace agreement with the Polisario guerrilla movement in early August 1979, under which it renounced all claim to the southern part of the Western Sahara, Morocco quickly occupied and administratively integrated the whole of the territory into Morocco proper.

Compared to the Middle East, the Maghrib is much more religiously unified with the Malikite rite of orthodox or Sunni Islam predominating. There are no indigenous Christian minorities and no important Islamic sects, except for the Kharijites of Jerba and the Mzabites of Algeria. Indigenous Jews constitute an insignificant and steadily diminishing minority. Because of this uniformity, North African Islam serves as an important common denominator transcending and mitigating the differences of tribe, language, and life style. Unlike any other historical or contemporary force, Islam remains paramount in all three countries notwithstanding the different policies toward religion and religious practice adopted by the various political leaders of the Maghrib.

By way of summary, we can identify eight principal characteristics of North African Islam which distinguish it somewhat from the Middle East and which provide that society with an important cohesive force and distinctive identity [adapted from Brown, 1966].

1. As already indicated and compared to the Arab Middle East, North African Islam demonstrates greater uniformity and has done so for centuries since the collapse of the Almohad Empire. For example, all North African Muslims are Sunni, and the vast majority follow the same Maliki school of Islamic law. The notable exceptions to this rule, as noted above, are the very small Mzabite community in South Central Algeria and the few remaining Kharijites on Jerba, an island off the east coast of Tunisia.

2. Similarly, unlike the Arab East, there are hardly any native Christian populations in the Maghrib. In fact, it was in the 1150s that the last handful of Christian dioceses disappeared.

3. Because of the above two historical developments, Islam constitutes the single most important denominator in North Africa today. In fact, it would not be an exaggeration to indicate that as a symbol of unity and identity, Islam is to the Maghrib what Arab nationalism is to the Middle East. In the way that a common Arabness can be used in the Arab East to overcome the differences between Sunnis, Shiites, and the many Christian denominations, so Islam plays the same

role in North Africa serving to transcend such basic differences as those between Arab and Berber.

4. From the late medieval period until the twentieth century, Muslim mysticism has flourished in North Africa in the form of mass religious brotherhoods led and personified by the *shaykh* or *marabout* (religious leader). The *Sufi* religious brotherhoods filled real social and political functions.

5. In the modern era these Muslim brotherhoods have begun to decline in importance. In the premodern period they served the useful purpose of extending Islam into the countryside, providing asylum, mediating between the tribes and the central government, and rallying political protest movements against the central government. But with modernization and the increased power of the central state apparatus, the former political role of the brotherhoods has been made obsolete. Likewise, within urban and more literate population centers the brotherhoods, representing a popular, irrational, and usually provincial form of Islam, are becoming less appealing.

6. The rapid decline of the brotherhoods in North Africa can be attributed in great part to the Islamic reformist movements that arrived in the Maghrib via the teachings of Muhammad Abduh (1849–1905) and his *salifiyya* movement, a movement which argued that the true Islam was that which was taught by the Prophet and the Elders (*salaf*). In all the three countries of North Africa, Islamic reformism led the attack against the brotherhoods, was in favor of expanding Arabic and Islamic education, sought to reform traditional religious education in order to make it more adaptable to modern needs, and, in general terms, fought against anything that smacked of assimilation. Because of the above, Islamic reformism in Morocco, Algeria, and Tunisia has been closely linked with early, preindependence nationalism.

7. Another striking phenomenon in North Africa today is related to the above: the decline of the old religious elite. As with the religious brotherhoods, the orthodox *ulama* (re-

ligious scholars) began to decline in power and prestige as a result of the modernization process which was somewhat accelerated by the colonial experience. Even where reformist *ulama* were directly involved in the preindependence nationalist struggle, as in Algeria, this was not enough to salvage their prestige or retrieve their position.

As a class in all three countries, the *ulama* have already lost much of their institutional base from which to exert power and influence. For all practical purposes they have lost control of education; they are quickly losing their last foothold in the legal profession with the *sharia* (religious) courts increasingly giving way to single, national court systems; and they have lost virtually all the perquisites coming from the administration of *habous* or religious trust properties.

8. Finally, in each of the three postindependence constitutions, Islam is designated as the state religion. The Algerian and Tunisian presidents must be Muslims, and in the Moroccan constitution, the king is given the title "commander of the faithful." There is virtually no antireligious or, to the extent that it is appropriate, anticlerical feeling in North Africa.

This seeming ethnoreligious uniformity should not be exaggerated, however, inasmuch as numerous internal diversities mark the North African human and social landscape. We have already noted how the Maghrib is geographically fragmented in ways which do not complement each other. Likewise, despite the overall pattern of homogeneity, there still persists important linguistic and cultural divisions. In socioeconomic terms as well, these disharmonies are reflected in the principal lifeways which the region supports. Six distinct rural patterns can be identified in the Maghrib. The first is the pure nomad of the desert found south of the Anti-Atlas and the Saharan Atlas. The second type is the seminomad of the steppe-desert found principally throughout the plateaus of Algeria north of the Saharan Atlas and in central Tunisia. A third rural pattern is that of the mountain transhumants or herders who bring their livestock down to the sheltering plains in winter and ascend to Alpine-like meadows in summer. Those found in the Middle Atlas of Morocco are a good example of this third type. In the fourth category are the sedentary Berberophone mountaineers. They cover all of the Rif and most of the High Atlas in Morocco, and there are more than 2.5 million of them in the mountains of Kabylia in central Algeria. These are both farmers and orchard-keepers who have terraced gardens on the slopes of steep mountains. Because of the enormous problem of overpopulation in these areas, Rifians and Kabyles have traditionally emigrated for seasonal labor or, more permanently, to the cities of Morocco, Algeria, and France. The fifth group is almost an unclassifiable large bloc of tribes and loosely organized groups found in the coastal plains and the hills of Morocco south and east of Casablanca and in many parts of eastern Algeria. This group is only now in the proces of permanently settling on the land. Many of them practice both pastoral activities and agriculture. The sixth and last of the important rural types is the authentic village life of North Africa. This is found in the old, settled areas of northeast Tunisia and along the Sahel of the country's eastern shore. It is here that one finds the highest degree of rural sophistication in the Maghrib.

For the great majority of those who live on the land— more than 60 percent—there is still great dependency on cereals, above all on wheat. While this crop has traditionally provided stable sustenance to the people and shown great resilience, the quantity of its yield has remained vulnerable to temporal-climatic conditions, especially the timing, frequency, and amount of rainfall. An excess of rain leaches the soil, taking nutrition below the reach of the roots, so that a wet year exhausts the soil for the following season as well. Similarly, the annual yield depends on the wind which, if it blows too hot or severely during the ripening, may ruin the harvest.

While the importance of wheat, and therefore of climate and soil, has changed little, those living on the land also have been affected by demographic and population forces that have shifted populations away from the land into the towns and cities. This movement often caused a change from wheat-exporting to wheat-importing economies even when allowance is made for changes in consumption patterns. The overall impact of increased population is accelerated as the delicate balance of a rural economy, trading the products of the pasture with those of the town and village, is broken down.

Like its rural patterns, North African urban life is diverse. There are first of all the traditional Islamic cities like Fez, Tunis, Rabat, Tetuan, and Tlemcen. These are old, urbane cities which possess a natively cultivated bourgeoisie. The best tradition of eastern Arabo-Islamic culture is to be found in these cities. A second group of cities are the coastal port towns like Algiers, Tangier, Oran, and Bejaia (Bougie), which possess no distinctive quality but simply reflect the pattern found among most Mediterranean port cities. They are normally cut off from their own culture and society and stand out as incongruously populated peninsulas detached from the heartland in a physical and spiritual sense. A third urban type quite distinct from the two above is that of a strategic regional center founded for economic or political purposes. Marrakesh in southwest Morocco and Constantine in eastern Algeria are two good examples of such cities. Finally, many new towns like Kenitra (formerly Port Lyautey), Annaba (formerly Bone), Skikda (formerly Philippeville), and Casablanca were created to serve European markets as well as smaller cities like Sétif in Algeria which were established for security reasons or to exploit natural resources.

Urbanization in North Africa must be distinguished from urbanism. The growth of population in the countryside has resulted in large scale internal migrations into towns and cities. Thus the movement into urban conglomerations owes more to demographic pressures in the rural areas than to rapid economic growth in the towns. Such population concentrations, however, do not become transformed into "modern" men exhibiting all the traits associated with urbanism such as "sophistication," tolerance of change, universalism, and impersonal relations. They are simply relocated from one physical space to another without necessarily undergoing a qualitative change in outlook, behavioral patterns, and the organizational networks which they create and in which they participate. This pattern of over-urbanization and under-urbanism in the Maghrib represents but one dimension of a larger phenomenon taking place throughout the Arab world. But even here, distinctions must be made between Tunisia, where a long tradition of urban life has existed in such cities as Tunis, Sfax, Sousse, and Kairouan, and Algeria, where there has been practically no urban history to be spoken of, with the notable exception of Tlemcen. Today's modern cities in Algeria are the creation of the French. Morocco stands somewhere in between, with Fez and Marrakesh representing the best example of traditionally established urban development, and Casablanca and Rabat being modern cities with minimal historic antecedents.

A summary of selected demographic, social, economic, agricultural, nutritional, and health indices for Morocco, Algeria, and Tunisia are presented in Table 1.

HISTORY

Indigenous Berber society has been subjected to five major foreign invasions and influences. The first conquest occurred around 1200 B.C. and lasted nearly a thousand years, bringing the Phoenicians and Carthaginians. Roman domination followed next, being firmly established with the destruction of Carthage in 146 B.C. and lasting for 650 years. There then followed the brief interlude (429–642) of the Vandals and Byzantine restoration. This was succeeded by

TABLE 1

Selected Demographic, Social, Economic, Agricultural,
Nutritional, and Health Indices for Morocco, Algeria,
and Tunisia (1976)

Indicator	Morocco	Algeria	Tunisia
Population (1976 estimate) (Million)	18	17.2	5.9
Crude Birth Rate (per 1,000)	47	49	37
Crude Death Rate (per 1,000)	16	17	12
Population Growth Rate (%)	2.9	3.0	2.4
Percent Urban	38	50	40
Estimated Infant Mortality Rate (per 1,000 live births)	130	125	100
Life Expectancy at Birth (years)	53	53	54
Gross National Product Per Capita (U.S.$)	280	530	350
Projected GNP Per Capita, 1985 (U.S.$)	430	1,500	540
Percent of Women Age 15 + Economically Active	12.6	2.9	5.5
Number of Acres of Arable Land Per Person	1.0	1.0	1.9
1974 Net Import of Cereal Grains (1,000 metric tons)	856	1,774	297
Health Workers and Health Infrastructure (per 10,000 in population)			
Physicians	0.7	1.2	1.6
Nurses	5	3.7	10.2
Midwives	0.08	0.4	14.3
Hospital Beds	14.4	28.1	23.6

SOURCE: Robert J. Lapham, "Population Policies in the Middle East and North Africa," *Middle East Studies Association Bulletin* (2) (May 1, 1977); 22, 24, Tables 1 and 2.

1,200 years of Arab predominance in Morocco. By 800 A.D. Arab supremacy reigned throughout the rest of the Maghrib. A Turkish regime was established in Algeria and Tunisia in the middle of the sixteenth century and continued in modified form until the nineteenth century when Euopean occupation occurred.

None of these successive foreign invasions managed to totally destroy the underlying fabric of Berber culture. The coming of the Arabs and Islam in the mid-seventh century did affect the Berbers culturally, however. In accepting Islam, for example, they took up many of the characteristics of Arab civilization, especially its language. Unlike earlier conquerors and later invaders, the Berbers seemingly surrendered and assimilated themselves to the Arabs. Yet the five principal external influences have not completely obliterated the cultural tenacity that still gives distinction and uniqueness to Berber life.

The whole of the Maghrib was brought under Arab control by 710. However, direct Arab rule by the Eastern caliphate over the Maghrib was terminated by the end of the eighth century, leaving the three states of North Africa to develop their own autonomous sociopolitical forms, at the local level at least.

In the three hundred years following the initial conquest of the Maghrib by the forces of the Arabo-Islamic world, a confused pattern of political rule, social forms, and religious movements emerged. What assumes lasting importance in this period, however, was the "slow assimilation of Islam by the masses of [North Africa] who were trying to adapt this or that tendency of the religion to the solution of local problems. The formal leadership was almost always external, the causes and slogans were Islamic, but the real issue was the social organization of Berbery and the development of a Maghribi personality" [Gallagher, 1963:49].

The eleventh century witnessed the emergence of the first

of three indigenous empires in the Maghrib which, during the next four centuries, established the foundation for the three states that were later to emerge with their own identities and histories.

The Almoravid empire (1042–1147) was established by Berber-speaking nomads from western Sahara and Mauritania. The Almoravids were the first dynasty to unify Morocco, and at one time their rule extended as far as Algiers. They established the historic link between the Maghrib and Muslim Spain which was to last two and a half centuries, bringing enormous benefits to North Africa and extending the life of Muslim Spain. It was also during this period that the Almoravids eliminated all heretical sects and imposed, with a permanent imprint, the Malikite school, a strict orthodox sect of Islam named after an eighth century religious leader of Medina, Malik Ibn Anas.

The second major indigenous empire to be established were the Almohads (1147–1269) who were the direct successors to the Almoravids. They were sedentary Berber mountaineers of the High Atlas who, in the fashion of their predecessors, were impelled by the visionary leadership of a puritanical religious teacher, Ibn Tumart (1076–1130). Probably the most significant political contribution of the Almohads was that they unified the Maghrib under a single home rule from Agadir (in Morocco) to Tripoli (in Libya) for the first and only time in history. In the areas of literature and philosophy as well, there was a lasting impact as attested to by the intellectual originality of such Islamic thinkers as Ibn Tufail and Ibn Rushd or, as he is more commonly known in the West, Averroes.

The capture of Marrakesh in 1269 by Merinid leader Abu Yusuf marks the end of the Almohad empire and the subsequent emergence of three separate Berber kingdoms: the Hafsids, a branch of the Almohad dynasty founded by one of their lieutenants, in the east (Tunis); the Zayanids or

Banu Abdul Wadides in the center (Tlemcen); and the Merinids in the west (Fez). Under the Merinids, Fez prospered, making it equal to any town in the world in terms of civility, culture, and refinement. Under the Hafsids, Tunis became the uncontested capital of Tunisia and an important center of Mediterranean commerce. While Christians of various nationalities lived and worked freely in the town, traditional Islamic learning was assiduously cultivated as well. During the Hafsid period, the Zitouna mosque became one of the foremost centers of learning in the Maghrib. The famous historian of the period, Ibn Khaldoun, studied in the Zitouna. Politically, the reign of the Hafsids marks the period when the country becomes recognizable as the forerunner of Tunisia today. The Zayanids ruled over a society that was essentially tribal, yet urban and civilized life developed in their realm as well. The Zayanid state, like the Merinid and to a lesser extent the Hafsid, profited from the administrative and artistic skills of Andalusian refugees in creating the rudiments of an administration and embellishing the capital, Tlemcen, with mosques and schools. During the Zayanid period, Tlemcen, the "pearl of the Maghrib," became for the first and only time the capital of an independent state.

The progressive initiative characterizing these separate Berber empires was virtually exhausted by 1500 when things had changed greatly. With the reconquest of Spain complete, it was the Iberian powers who began to intervene in North Africa and establish coastal enclaves, some founded as early as 1415 when the Portuguese got a foothold in Ceuta. Although it was able to avoid direct Ottoman rule, which Algeria and Tunisia began to experience by the mid-sixteenth century, Morocco was the victim of its own internal dissention, cultural stagnation, and military impotence vis-à-vis Spain and other European powers. Although Turkish rule never really took hold in Algeria and Tunisia, especially in the countryside where tribalism continued to be the most important feature of social organization, both countries experienced the same political and social stagnation that Morocco was manifesting, thus setting the stage for the full-blown intervention of the European powers beginning with the French conquest of Algeria in 1830 [unless otherwise indicated, the above discussion on land, people, and history is adapted from Gallagher, 1963].

EUROPEAN COLONIZATION

Modern colonialism is essentially a European phenomenon, an enterprise of expansion and domination spawned by the combined effects of rational bourgeois capitalism, demographic pressures, and power struggles among the European nation-states. All three states of North Africa were subjected to such colonial domination, and thus none of their political traditions and institutions have been spared the tumult of assault, distortion, and ultimate redefinition. Indeed, the problems of development and decay in the area are intimately associated with European participation in the destinies of the Maghrib world.

While European rule in the Maghrib varied according to the kinds of rules who came (French or Spanish, for example), the time the occupation took place, and the nature of the country or the portion of the country occupied, the overall process in all three countries was remarkably similar, notwithstanding the different types of colonial administrations established. French administrators and colonial settlers sought to implant the civilization of the metropolitan country. In their efforts they were supported by the military, forever remained outsiders, and enjoyed a privileged position vis-à-vis the native population.

More than 90 percent of the population of the Maghrib was colonized by France, with only northern Morocco escap-

TRANSPORTATION
—

TRANS-ACTION
1-9:4
BECAME: SOCIETY, WITH

TRAFFIC WORLD
—

BECAME: FAMILY HEALTH

ing this pattern and administered instead by a Spanish protectorate. In addition, this French colonization was intense and far reaching, more so in Algeria than Morocco, but pervasive throughout nonetheless. Algeria was conquered for all practical purposes in 1830, and French protectorates were established in Tunisia and Morocco in 1881 and 1912, respectively. French rule lasted 132 years in Algeria (1962), 75 years in Tunisia (1956), and 44 years in Morocco (1956). Algeria suffered the bulk of North Africa's settler population. At its height (1955), the European population constituted 13 percent of the total Algerian population and between 6 and 8 percent in Morocco and Tunisia. No comparable influx and presence of white settler society could be found outside Israel, South Africa, and Rhodesia. In terms of colonialism's impact on the land, settlers appropriated 27 percent of Algeria's arable lands (more than 7 million acres), 21 percent of Tunisia's arable lands (2 million acres), and 7 percent of Morocco's (2.5 million acres). Algeria constituted an integral part of France, whereas Tunisia and Morocco, as protectorates, preserved substantial elements of their indigenous precolonial governments, albeit in emasculated form. Protectorate status should not be distorted, however, for in both countries French administrators ended up controlling the all-important policy-making process in internal as well as external affairs. Under the nominal authority of the native head of state (the bey in Tunisia, the sultan in Morocco), French directors, supervised by the resident general, established new administrations which in effect were carbon copies of modern French ministries. The myth of the protectorate was not without its benefits, however, for it did help insure the survival of traditional elites in both countries. For the most part, the French preserved traditional institutions in Morocco and Tunisia, including, for example, the *habous* foundations. Other examples include the survival of the ancient mosque-universities in Tunis (Zitouna) and Fez (Qarawiyin), the retention of traditional mechanisms regulating urban commerce, and the continuing high status of traditional families in Tunisia and Morocco.

In terms of administrative practice, the main trend of the colonial experience was the shifting of the basic structures of the society from tribal forms of solidarity to more differentiated social structures. In societal terms colonialism caused increasing differentiation, tribal erosion, rural exodus, and emigration of thousands of people to Europe.

It may be helpful for our subsequent analysis of the country-by-country colonial experiences to identify three distinct forms of colonialism in North Africa based on essentially economic criteria. Segmented colonialism, best represented by the experience of Morocco, involves a limited yet highly visible economic domination without, however, destroying the basic political and cultural order. The case of Tunisia represents a form of instrumental colonialism which also involves exclusive economic domination and exploitation, but which does not hesitate, when necessary, to intervene in other levels of society. Finally, total colonialism, as in Algeria, constitutes unrestrained domination of the whole society at all levels, based upon the negation of the social, cultural, and economic order of the colonized country.

ALGERIA: TOTAL COLONIALISM

The initial French conquest of Algeria was relatively easy. French troops left Toulon on May 25, 1830, landed in Algeria on June 14, and by July 5, Algiers had capitulated. Another four decades, however, were needed before all of Algeria was "pacified" under French control. Most resistance in the countryside, like that led by the youthful nationalist, Emir Abd al-Kader, was eventually suppressed, viciously at times, so that by 1847 all but the mountains of Kabylia were brought under French authority. In Kabylia there was stubborn and bloody resistance, and official control was not declared until 1857. Even then, revolts took place in 1864, and a general uprising, following a grievous famine, occurred in 1871, all of which were brutally put down, leaving the country prostrate and its population virtually decimated.

At the end of the first fifty years of French occupation, Muslims in Algeria had lost not only their freedom but also their land. By 1833, for example, *habous* land had been officially appropriated. A decade later a law was passed dividing the communally held lands (*arsh*) and personalized property holdings. Such measures inevitably destroyed tribal authority while facilitating the sale of land by individuals. To encourage settlement authorities in Paris offered French settlers free transportation, land, seed, and livestock. It was estimated that by the early 1850s more than 150,000 Europeans had settled permanently in Algeria. With the collapse of the Second Empire following the Franco-Prussian war in 1870, Algeria's political status was tied even more closely to metropolitan France. The country was administratively divided into three departments (Constantine, Algiers, and Oran)—an area containing more than 90 percent of the total population and covering practically the whole of the country's productive land. Paris appointed a governor general who had the power to legislate by decree thus enabling him to control the application of, or altogether withhold, metropolitan legislation. Each department was headed by a prefect who was directly responsible to the French ministry of the interior. With strong backing from French officialdom, Algeria's European settlers gained in strength and were able to exercise vast influence on the machinery of government: they could determine policies, influence the enactment and execution of laws, and control the appointment of high officials of the administration.

The political and personal status of Algerian Muslims

were likewise deeply affected. For a while, the Arab tribes were allowed to govern themselves, with chiefs selected and approved by officers of the *Bureaux Arabes,* who were not unsympathetic to Algerian culture and customs as reflected in their learning of Arabic, native culture, and habits. However, there was constant and heavy pressure by the colon settlers or *pieds noirs* ("black feet") to remove the tribes from military control, extend the territory under civilian authority, and put the natives under administrators who would be more susceptible to settler influence.

An 1865 law declared that henceforth native Muslims were to be considered as Frenchmen under the condition that to attain full citizenship and the right to vote, Algerian Muslims had to follow French civil law. In effect, what this meant was that for an Algerian to become a French citizen he had to disavow his "personal status" which, in the Muslim context, was tantamount to abandoning the *sharia* code and renouncing one's Muslim identity. Not surprisingly, by the early 1930s only 2,000 or so Algerian Muslims had chosen French citizenship under such conditions.

Perhaps the most effective and onerous device for governing the Muslim population was the *Code de L'Indigénat,* which was in effect from 1881 to 1944. Under these laws, for example, an Algerian Muslim was forbidden to speak against France and the government, prohibited in keeping stray animals for more than twenty-four hours, forbidden to exercise the profession of elementary teaching without proper authorization, and not permitted to travel from one place to another within Algeria without a visaed permit. Punishment for such crimes and others, including delay in paying taxes, giving shelter to strangers without permission, or holding gatherings of more than twenty persons, ranged from payment of fines, to confiscation of property, to indefinite administrative internment.

By the turn of the century, Algerian Muslims had been

reduced from relative prosperity to economic, social, and cultural inferiority. Three million inhabitants had died, tribes had been broken up, and the traditional economy was radically altered during the prolonged "civilizing" campaigns. In particular, the production of wine for export had replaced the traditional production of cereals for domestic consumption. Virtually the whole of Algeria's traditional economic structure and land use practices were dislocated as a consequence of French colonial policy with its property laws, its sequestrations of land after the early revolts, its expropriations, its forestry laws, its regulations concerning pasture lands, and a host of other measures that were either forced upon the administration or inspired by its policy of giving preferential considerations to the interests of the Europeans.

Under such conditions of near total decimation of native society, the intermittent attempts at incremental political and social reforms appeared inconsequential. So long as the settler population remained *de facto* rulers of Algeria, metropolitan-inspired reform legislation seemed doomed. Shortly before World War II, for example, the Popular Front government of Leon Blum sponsored a reform bill (Blum-Viollette Reform Bill) intended to grant French citizenship to over 20,000 Algerian Muslims. Yet due to the concerted opposition of the European settlers, the bill was not even allowed to be voted upon in parliament. Another and final attempt to resolve this problem was made in 1947 with the proclamation of the so-called "Statute for Algeria" which introduced a new formula based on a policy of "integration." This law recognized Algeria's "dual" status wherein the country remained "part of France" while maintaining its separate Muslim identity. Under such conditions Muslims were to be granted French citizenship without, however, infringing upon their personal status or forcing the abandonment of the *sharia* code. In addition, religious instruction was to be protected against state interference and the Arabic language was to be taught in the Muslim schools. Politically Algerians were finally given the right to vote but on a basis of communal equality with the Europeans and not proportionate to the population. As in the past the statute attempt failed. Blocked by the powerful and well-organized opposition of the settlers, the law's provisions were never fully or properly carried out. Not surprisingly, therefore, elections held in 1948 resulted in continued domination by the European minority. For all practical purposes this destroyed the last hope for any lasting solution and reinforced the base of the revolution which finally broke out in 1954.

TUNISIA: INSTRUMENTAL COLONIALISM

The French colonial experience in Tunisia, while not "benign," was nonetheless free of the disruptive societal transformations which took place in neighboring Algeria. Indeed, local social structures, culture, leadership, and institutions remained relatively immune from French colonial practices. If anything, these institutions were supported and strengthened under the French protectorate which was imposed on the country in the Treaty of Kassar Said, also known as the Treaty of Bardo, signed on May 12, 1881. Under its terms, the bey of Tunis agreed to the "voluntary limitation" of the external sovereignty of Tunisia for a "temporary but indefinite period." France was empowered to act in a sovereign manner in all external Tunisian affairs and in matters relating to the defense of the country. The resident general of France was designated as the sovereign's foreign minister. In 1883, under the imposed terms of the Treaty of La Marsa, Tunisian sovereignty was relinquished in the domestic sphere as well, as the French assumed supervision and control of the country's internal authority via another one-sided treaty arrangement. Although the traditional hierarchy of the beylical government was preserved, a separate parallel French administration was established which quickly acquired all effective control in the state. The bey was reduced to a figurehead, and all real power passed to a French resident general.

At the local level as well, the idea of parallelism and *contrôle*, or supervision, was being implemented. The *qaid*, or traditional local executive, for example, was kept in authority, but his activities were closely supervised by *contrôleurs civils* (civil supervisors) from 1884 on. In time, these colonial officials exceeded their assigned functions of observation, comment, and approval and usurped the prestige and eventually even the functions of the Tunisian officials themselves. However efficient this parallel administrative system of the protectorate may have been, it basically undermined national self-confidence and made progress towards a healthy development that much more difficult to achieve.

Although the cruelty with which land was appropriated and the tribal system broken in Algeria was not repeated in Tunisia, French administration nevertheless put the European settlers' interests first and subjected Tunisia to "reforms" that were clearly not in the interest of the Muslim population. The *habous* land, for example, though not directly confiscated, was made legally salable. Sale to Europeans was simplified by requiring individual landholdings to be registered. Inevitably, as land was bought up by settlers, the rural Muslim population sank into much the same destitution as the neighboring Algerian population. Administrative offices and positions were denied to Tunisians until after the First World War although in theory such offices were opened equally to Tunisian and European civil servants. As happened in Algeria, the settler population repeatedly obstructed reforms granting Tunisians equal rights with Europeans as they held fast to their control of the political and economic life of the country. What was different in Tunisia, however, was that unlike their counterparts in Algeria the Europeans were unable for long to suppress the rise and rapid spread of Tunisian nationalism.

On balance, however, the French colonial experience in Tunisia was moderated in great part by the process of modernization which had already been underway prior to the French arrival. The local government of the Ottoman bey, for example, was already modernized and reinvigorated by a reformist-minded prime minister. Local government was relatively ordered and effective, elements of modern education, such as the Sadiqi College, were already in evidence. The French found a society in the early stages of modernization through which it sought to rule by discreet and indirect means through the agent of the bey, assisted by French *contrôleurs civils*. French military presence, so pronounced in Algeria and Morocco, was virtually absent in the country or the administration in Tunisia. Even the French settler population, which never reached more than 7 percent of the total Tunisian population, managed to limit its economic and commercial penetration of the country, leaving alone, for example, the fertile and commercially prosperous area of the Sahel along the central eastern coast of the country.

Perhaps the most serious charge than can be levelled against the protectorate was the insufficient effort made in education. The French instituted a dual educational system, one part of which was wholly French with standards equated to those in the homeland, the other a mixed Franco-Arab education. The latter was admittedly of lower quality, and although there was never segregation of any kind, the spirit behind the duality served to preserve a European minority and to dispense an inferior brand of instruction to the native population. Yet, despite this qualitative limitation, the French-instituted bilingual system of Arabic and French language instruction, which was discouraged in Algeria and never really developed in the brief protectorate period in Morocco, enabled Tunisia's educated elite to possess bilingual cultural and language skills, reinforced in their university training in France, which became so necessary in the upcoming nationalist struggle for independence and the subsequent modernization of the country.

MOROCCO: SEGMENTED COLONIALISM

Until 1894, Morocco remained viable under the rule of a strong and effective sultan, Moulay Hassan (1873–1894), who, among other things, maintained internal order and kept the country's finances on a relatively sound footing thanks in part to a flourishing export trade. Moreover, Moulay obtained the diplomatic assistance of Britain in his attempt to inhibit the annexationist ambitions of France and Spain. Relatively immuned from outside intervention, the dynamic sultan built up an army, reestablished authority in the Alawi Sharifian empire, which had been established in 1666, and reinstated financial order.

With his death, however, the country realized immediate difficulties because of the prodigality and mismanagement of Moulay's son and successor, Abd al-Aziz (1894–1908), a young and weak ruler. Not even the competence and political integrity of the new sultan's prime minister, Grand Vizier Ba Ahmed, was able to reverse the rapid economic and political deterioration of the country. With Ba Ahmed's death in 1900, the sultan's extravagant life style, eccentric and foolish policies turned what was an otherwise healthy financial situation into a virtual disaster in which the treasury was nearly empty and domestic violence widespread. In financial chaos, the throne had to borrow and quickly went into severe debt. No longer able to resist European pressures and creditors, the country's internal sovereignty began to come into question. The intrigues and maneuvers of foreign agents who ill advised Aziz in economic and financial matters virtually sealed the coffin on Moroccan autonomy. By 1908, the revolt against Aziz had become general as he was accused of having abandoned Morocco to foreigners and foreign financial interests. Overwhelmed from all sides, Aziz gave up the throne and allowed his brother, Moulay Hafid (1908–1912), to succeed him.

The new Sultan, however, was in no better position to resist European political and economic interests than his brother and, in fact, further indebted the country in a futile attempt to salvage its enormous debts. At the same time, dissident tribes in Fez besieged him, and he turned to France for military, political, and economic assistance. The conditions under which French intervention occurred were indeed to be exorbitant—nothing less than the relinquishment of Moroccan political independence. This was formalized in the Treaty of Fez, signed by France and Morocco on March 30, 1912, formally establishing the protectorate.

Nonetheless, the complete pacification of the country took nearly a quarter of a century to accomplish before the vigorous opposition in the Anti-Atlas was finally overcome. The French pacification of Morocco was carried out in four principal stages. Between 1912 and 1914, the French were involved in the first phase of subjugating the *bled al-makhzen,* that part of the country traditionally under the sultan's control. This was followed by the pacification of the Middle Atlas which lasted until 1920. The third phase, from 1921 to 1926, involved the enormously costly, in human and material terms, subjugation of Abd al-Krim and his forces in the Rif war. Finally, from 1930 to 1934, a series of military operations wiped out the last pockets of resistance in the High Atlas, Anti-Atlas, and on the edges of the Sahara. Of the three Maghribi states, only in Morocco could one identify a "continuity of resistance," for when the traditional tribal battles and country-side wars terminated, an urbanized version of nationalist resistance immediately emerged, bent on the same eventual goal of freedom for Morocco.

While modeled on the legal status established in Tunisia, the protectorate in Morocco dealt a more severe blow to national sovereignty inasmuch as the Fez treaty granted France the power and sole responsibility for all reforms, national defense, foreign affairs, and economic and financial matters. This impact was not lessened by the fact that the French committed themselves to guaranteeing the sultan's "religious condition and prestige" and to lend constant support to his person and throne.

The basic structure of the sultan's government was retained; indeed, the feudal elements in Moroccan society were encouraged, and the great families maintained their powerful positions. No separate administrative structure was established alongside that of the sultan as had been done in Tunisia. Instead, a departmental system was created as an administrative substructure run exclusively by French officials. Official legislation and decrees were signed by the sultan and promulgated in his name, leaving him at the center of public life and at least nominally the source of authority in the country.

In Morocco as in Tunisia, French authority was represented in the person of a resident general. Marshal Lyautey, Morocco's first and probably most brilliant resident general (1912–1925), brought with him a not untypical romantic, paternalistic, but in the final analysis, racist image of the "valient," "simple," "loyal," and "noble" savage that constituted the Moroccan "native" in the eyes of many French settlers and administrators. It was this so-called romanticized image of Morocco and Moroccans, which never really had its counterpart in Algeria and Tunisia, that explains in part the support provided by the protectorate for native and traditional institutions which simply helped to retain many medieval social structures and propped up and confirmed some of the great feudal families.

Extensive colonization in Morocco came late, since actual

pacification of the country was not really achieved until the 1930s. At this point, major concessions were given to large French companies and state-owned combines. Unlike in Algeria, the colonizers were mostly lower-middle-class professionals who emigrated to Morocco to get better-paying jobs, mostly in business and administration. Marshal Lyautey, consistent with his perceptions of native society, established a policy of preservation aimed at perpetuating the social customs and traditions of the Moroccan population and protecting it from the transforming influences of Europe. (He instituted complete separation between the *medinas* [the native towns] and the European sections of the major cities, for example.)

Lyautey's patriarchal policy of total one-man control was facilitated in part by the role the army played throughout most of the forty-three years of the protectorate. Particularly in rural Morocco and the Berber regions, the army stayed on to serve the administration after pacification had taken place.

Unlike what happened under French colonialism in Algeria, political and social institutions in Morocco were left intact. This meant, as noted above, that traditionally privileged classes were preserved, especially the commercially and culturally dominant Arab bourgeoisie in the cities of Fez and Rabat and the Berber tribal notables of the countryside. Similarly, internal social evolution was modest and the social elites were neither infused with fresh blood by upwardly mobile lower groups, nor did many of them receive a modern French education or achieve access to modern administrative and professional careers as, for example, had occurred in Tunisia. As a consequence, employment in government became overwhelmingly French. For example, in 1945, Moroccans occupied only 26 percent of 20,492 administrative jobs and these mostly at the bottom of the administrative ladder. Similarly, in the period 1912–1955, only approximately one thousand Moroccans had successfully completed modern secondary education and obtained the French baccalaureat. In addition, among those who did receive French education, urban Arabs, for the most part, attended one set of French-controlled schools in Fez and Rabat, while the sons of Berber notables attended another, thus exascerbating existing social cleavages. A number of sons of Berber rural families attended the French military academy in Meknès and remained disturbingly loyal to French rule until the eve of independence itself [Kerr, 1976:384–85].

Despite virtually continuous Moroccan resistance to French domination, it was not until the late 1930s that small numbers of upper class intellectuals began to organize the first political groups and oppositional movements. Consistent with their westernized background, these groups demanded legal and administrative reform not unlike their Tunisian counterparts. The calls for reform were transformed into demands for complete independence only with the collapse of France and the Allied landing in North Africa in 1942. The *Istiqlal* (independence) Party drew up a formal manifesto in January 1944 just one month after its formation in December 1943. As in Tunisia, French reaction to nationalist demands alternated between partial concession and repression. Frustrated by French indecision, the nationalist resistance went underground in 1952, and open rebellion against France was subsequently declared.

PREINDEPENDENCE NATIONALIST MOVEMENTS

The nationalist movements of North Africa emerged as a consequence of two powerful forces, one essentially negative, the other positive. On one hand, Maghribi nationalism began as a direct reaction to Western colonial rule and, on the other, was influenced by and related to the wider revival of Arab nationalist consciousness that made itself felt in the mid-nineteenth century. The particular form of this nationalist expression, however, was decisively European in ideology, terminology, and structural organization, with French leftist political thought being particularly influential. Because of this origin, however, North African nationalism has continued to display dual and sometimes conflicting tendencies. That is, the traditionalist, religious, oriental, and purely Arabic components vie with the modernist, secular, occidental, and bilingual elements of Maghribi nationalism, resulting in a serious ideological cleavage which has yet to be resolved in a manner satisfactory to both masses and elites alike.

In all three states of the Maghrib, the nationalist response to the colonial situation assumed relatively similar forms. The *liberal assimilationists,* sons of the old, traditional elite who admired and imitated the colonial rulers, assimilated some of their styles and values, and accepted their rules of the game. This first-generation nationalist elite proved inadequate however, because they were never really accepted by the colonialists or, for that matter, by their own masses and simply ended up as privileged Westernized natives virtually cutoff from their own society. Under such conditions, no real reconciliation between nationalist aspirations and colonialist designs could take place.

A second group of elites, both older and contemporaries of the liberal assimilationists, were *traditionalists* who assumed a nationalitarian-scripturalist orientation. This persepective was advocated by the learned, scholarly, and urban families, which historically had constituted a distinctive status group. They called for a reaffirmation of national, cultural, and religious integrity in the face of Western colonial domination. This group was also the first during colonialism to call for the maintenance of a national personality usually by stressing the use, revision, and celebration of the Islamic heritage (scripturalism), and by emphasizing Arabism as a language, culture, and common history (nationalitarianism). This view defined the colonial situation in essentially spiritual and cultural terms which helps explain the focus on religious and cultural revivalism as the basis for a nationalist salvation. These views were held, for example, by such men as Allal al-Fassi in Morocco, Shaykh Abdelhamid Ben Badis in Algeria, and Abdel Aziz Thaalbi in Tunisia. In the final analysis, however, this traditionalist anticolonialism posture proved ineffectual in challenging the hegemony of the colonial presence. More important, perhaps, it proved incapable of constructing a new political culture that could meet the challenge of the West.

A third and ultimately decisive group were the *populists* who, while they were educated and trained in European schools and environments and sought to recreate in their societies the liberal trends formed in the Europe of the bourgeois revolutions, rebelled against the colonial status quo and appealed for mass mobilization against foreign domination. Men like Tunisia's Bourguiba, Algeria's Messali, and the early Ben Barka of Morocco were representative of the populist elite who had grown "frustrated by the previous generation's failure to effect legalism and parliamentarism." Unlike the traditionalists, the populists had a broader base of support, higher level of education, and a more cosmopolitan outlook. And unlike the assimilationists, the populists were much more determined to attack and oppose the colonial system and foreign domination. In essence these were secularists with a modernizing view of political change who, while profoundly marked by a nationalist ideology and political activism, were much influenced by Europe as a model for their own growth and hence were committed to a gradual, evolutionary form of social change. Yet their commitment to European principles exposed the populists to certain inherent contradictions, so that while they were militant in their struggle against France, they tended to be somewhat reconciliatory once in power. "Given the context from which they matured and emerged—the absence of parliamentary life, less differentiated societies, and a total, as opposed to a marginal, form of politics—[the populists were] encouraged to become authoritarian and patrimonial in style, populist in language, and gradualist in methods of government" [Hermassi, 1972: 96].

A fourth category of elite types emerged in the post-independence period. Emanating essentially from the *radical intelligentsia* and workers, this most recent nationalist orientation calls for mass mobilization and the radical restructuring of indigenous society. Men like Mohammed Harbi of Algeria, Ahmad Ben Salah of Tunisia, and the late Mehdi Ben Barka "all have tended to take the infrastructure of dependency of their societies much more seriously than did their predecessors." This orientation has only recently appeared, however, and even today its influence is indirect and its specific delineations uncertain. The populists, who were deeply involved in the preindependence nationalist struggle and who successfully overthrew colonial rule, most appropriately deserve the label of "nationalist" elite [These nationalist operations are adapted from Hermassi, 1972:91–92].

MOROCCO

Preprotectorate Morocco had its traditional elite; men from the great bourgeois families from Fez and elsewhere who subscribed to a nationalitarian-scripturalist orientation. Although desirous of independence, they eventually had to capitulate to French demands and reluctantly accepted their status. Between 1925 and 1930, another younger group of newly educated elites—populists—frustrated and embittered by French presence, found strong psychological and political support from the traditional elite. This group became increasingly formidable once this sense of national disaffection spread down to skilled craftsmen in the towns who themselves were beginning to feel the economic pinch of strong competition from manufactured goods introduced by the colonialists. Hence the union of the frustrated traditional elite, the radicalized younger elite, and the disaffected lower middle class constituted a formidable nationalist front with an urbanized focus.

The nationalist crisis officially broke out with the infamous Berber *dahir* or decree of May 16, 1930. The *dahir* was issued in Rabat ostensibly setting up customary tribunals in Berber-populated parts of the country to deal with civil cases. The decree also established a complete system of penal and criminal justice based on French law and deliberately removed both systems from the jurisdiction of the *makhzen* (monarchical authority). The French justified such a reform on the need to provide formal recognition to the Berber customary law, a loose body of tribal rules conforming with, and supplementary to, Quranic law. Yet this was transparently a colonial pretext to facilitate French control of the country by creating an artificial division between the Arabs and Berbers while supposedly winning over the support of the Berbers.

Incipient nationalist forces representing both traditionalists like Allel al-Fassi and westernized intellectuals like Ahmed Balafrej immediately and vigorously protested the decree which they viewed for what in fact it was: a blatant attempt at divide-and-rule. To their cause they immediately attracted the skilled craftsmen and shopkeepers of the towns. While French authorities sought to water down the implications of the dahir, the damage had already been done, and the sense of nationalist consciousness among Morocco's youth was already well awakened.

In May 1934, the *Kutlah al-Amal al-Watani*, or *Comité d'Action Marocaine* was set up and represented the first overtly nationalist party in the country. The comité published *Maghreb* in Paris and *L'Action du Peuple* in Fez, both of which served as sounding boards for the articulation of grievances against the residency. The *comité* was reformist in orientation since its demands did not include the elimination of the protectorate but instead called for respect for the Treaty of Fez, the ending of direct administration, administrative and judicial unity for all of Morocco, and the direct participation of Moroccans in the exercise of power. The *comité*, in presenting their *Plan de Réformes Marocaines* to the sultan, the resident general, and the premier of France, operated from an essentially evolutionary perspective; that is, working peacefully, but unsuccessfully, for reforms within the framework of the protectorate.

With the French dissolution of the *comité* in 1937, there was no real effective political organization leading the nationalist movement until the formation of the Istiqlal Party in 1943. The Istiqlal demanded full freedom for Morocco, with a constitutional form of government under Sultan Ben Youssef (later Mohammed V), who supported the nationalist movement.

After World War II the Istiqlal was joined by two other parties as contenders for the status of *the* nationalist party: the Democratic Independence Party (PDI), a splinter party from the Istiqlal, and the Communist Party which had very little support. The Istiqlal, with strong support in the towns and in tacit alliance with the throne, was being challenged by feudal chiefs, some traditionalist elements in the cities, and heads of some religious brotherhoods. Strong opposition was particularly evident among the conservative tribesmen of Morocco, who tended to concentrate their resistance to reform along western lines around Thami al-Glawi, the Pasha of Marrakesh.

From 1947 to 1951, the most significant event was the modest transformation of the Istiqlal from an elite to a mass party with independence as its overwhelming objective. When the Istiqlal-throne alliance became more overt and began to challenge French hegemony in the country, the colonial authorities instituted a series of harsh, repressive measures including, on August 20, 1953, deposing the sultan and exiling him first to Corsica and later to Madagascar and replacing him with a docile relative. The deportation catalyzed the nationalist movement into an all-out fight for freedom and independence. Indeed, this act coalesced the nation unlike anything before or since. At the popular level reactions were totally unanticipated. The king became a martyr and a saint in the eyes of the masses and his *baraka* (religiously inspired charisma) forever insured.

Incipient guerrilla warfare broke out following the sultan's deportation and the virtual destruction of the major political groupings. Widespread violence was avoided by the fact that a relatively quick political settlement was achieved.

The return from exile on November 6, 1955, of Mohammad V, in the midst of genuinely indescribable enthusiasm, constituted the virtual end of colonial rule in Morocco. It was finalized on March 2, 1956, when the country was formally declared independent. The Moroccan masses, whom the Istiqlal had not politically educated, believed in the king's traditional *baraka,* while the diverse forces of modern nationalism looked to him to satisfy their demands for a national government. He was the one leader whose title to rule rested on sufficiently diverse modern and traditional grounds to satisfy all sectors of the heterogeneous elite. Thus the emergence of the monarchy as the means to independence was achieved at the expense of the national elite who were forced into a secondary role. Indeed, Morocco is unique in the Middle East and North Africa in that the struggle for independence centered around the capture, revival, and renovation of a traditional institution, the monarchy.

TUNISIA

Tunisia was the first of the three North African countries to be influenced by modern nationalism. It was exposed to modernity earlier and experienced its own brief modernist renaissance in the 1850s. Although the first nationalist sentiments were expressed in the form of an Islamic renewal, its impact was slight. A secular stream found institutional expression in the Sadiqi College, which was established prior to the protectorate in 1875 and eventually constituted the principal educational source of the later reformist-minded Tunisian nationalists.

In 1905, the Young Tunisian Movement emerged from the common Sadiqi experience. Borrowing from the Young Turk movement of the decaying Ottoman Empire, the Young Tunisians represented the liberal assimilationist position of the first generation nationalist elite in the Maghrib. Characteristic of the assimilationist generation, the Young Tunisians were reformist not revolutionary in temperament and design. The demands they put forward were for better education, combining French and Arabic cultures, and access for Tunisians to government. While they varied in the emphasis they attached to Arabic and to French cultures, they all drew to some extent on the two. The Evolutionist Party they founded was peopled by the young, Europeanized professional middle class of Tunis; they commanded no national support or mass following, and their demands were framed within the limits of the protectorate which they sought to modify but not overthrow.

The year 1911 witnessed the first grass-roots expression of nationalist sentiment when tensions between Tunisians and the growing European settler population resulted in riots. Yet even here the Young Tunisians were essentially representative of prenationalist tendencies. Inasmuch as theirs was not a mass movement, they had no identifiable ideology or political doctrine of wide, popular appeal, and mutual ties between the elite and the population at large hardly existed.

The achievement of independence in eastern Arab countries after the First World War, and the example of the nationalist movement in Egypt, inspired Tunisians with a greater national consciousness and in February 1920, a new party called the Liberal Constitutional Party or, more popularly known by the Arabic word for constitution (*destour*), the Destourians, was formed under the leadership of Shaykh al-Thaalbi, one of the founders of the prewar Young Tunisians. The rise of the Destour marked a new moment in Tunisian nationalism, that of traditionalistic anticolonialism.

Destourian nationalist activity took place between the years 1920 and 1934 and included a call for a self-governing constitutional regime with a legislative assembly. The party was made up essentially of middle class urbanites who tended, however, to resemble bourgeoisie in traditional and semitraditional societies in that most were conservative, property-conscious, family-oriented, and devoutly religious individuals. As a bourgeois pressure group, the Destour lacked the coordination and persistence to gain piecemeal reforms; and it did not yet have the force of a mass party. The old generation of Destourians did little to capture the imagination of the new adherents, nor did they provide the dynamism of a revolutionary party. Internally split along generational lines and at the virtual mercy of the protectorate, the Destour was unable to effect meaningful change. But because the party was the obvious channel of protest, it recruited young men who, in the next decade, took over the movement and broke away and in March 1934, formed the Neo-Destour Party. Within a few years, the Neo-Destour appropriated the leadership of the nationalist movement.

The principal force behind the new party's creation was a thirty-one-year-old French-trained lawyer, Habib Bourguiba, who was eventually to lead Tunisia to independence and, in the process, earn the label, "father of his country." Bourguiba and his generation, trained in French universities in the twenties, represented the populist mode of nationalist consciousness. They inherited from the Young Tunisians a strong faith in liberal France and in its economic and cultural innovations, while from the old Destour they stole the banner of anticolonialism. What they reacted against was not the French presence as such, but rather the relationship of subordination it implied [Hermassi, 1972].

In his socioeconomic background, education, and professional training, Habib Bourguiba was representative of the Neo-Destour leadership. Born in 1903 at Monastir in the Sahel of middle class parents, he was educated as a lawyer, getting his professional degree from the Sorbonne. During his French educational experience, he developed impressive skills in writing and oratory which served him well as a political organizer and publicist. In 1932, for example, after arguing cases and contributing to the Destour journal, he founded his own publication, *L'Action Tunisienne.*

Unlike the old Destour, the Neo-Destourians were secular nationalists who were not, however, averse to using religion as a political weapon on occasions. Significantly, the younger nationalists broke away from the "traditional" bourgeoisie of Tunis and turned instead to the masses throughout the country for support. The Neo-Destour was committed to nationalist independence as well as to the modernization of the country via extensive grass-roots organization and political education and mobilization. The party's efforts were unchallenged by other nationalist groups and failed to be impeded by French attempts at occasional repression, exile of leaders, and other paralegal means of suppressing the nationalist movement.

The nationalist movement did not assume a violent dimension in Tunisia until 1954 when groups of guerrillas or *fellaghas* began to operate in the countryside tying down in the process nearly 70,000 French troops. Finally, by June 1955, with its hands full in Algeria, Morocco, and Indochina, the French government, under the premiership of Pierre Mendès-France, offered full internal autonomy to the country. Less than a year later, on March 20, 1956, Tunisian independence was formally declared.

In the brief period between June 1955 and March 1956, certain internal policy splits within the Neo-Destour began to emerge. Specifically, Bourguiba, the "Supreme Warrior," pursued a policy of gradualism or Bourguibism, as it was later to be known, in which the status of autonomy was viewed as a useful, indeed necessary, step towards eventual full independence. Opposition to this view came from the secretary-general of the party, Salah Ben Youssef, whose position was overturned, however, in a party congress held in fall 1955. This policy conflict which masked more serious ideological differences was later to reappear in a more pernicious form after independence.

ALGERIA

The Algerian nationalist movement may be divided into four distinct historical phases: 1. 1830–1870, the era of old nationalism; 2. 1870–1920, the crucial half century that saw the eclipse of rural and urban society; 3. 1920–1954, the period when an urban-based nationalist movement arose and gradually shifted from collaboration to radical opposition; and 4. 1954–1962, the final stage of mass-based revolutionary violence leading to formal independence in July 1962.

The stubborn revolt of the Algerian chief, Emir Abd al-Kader, against the imposition of French colonial rule in the 1830s provides more than simply the heroic opposition of a doomed but brave native leadership; rather, it may be argued that Abd al-Kader's defense of his country constituted the first basis for national unification and for central authority. Although it was ephemeral and was stimulated by the colonial domination, it did provide a first, albeit premature, necessary step to eventual nationalist identity in a society otherwise impervious to political unification. This assessment is based upon his attempt to build cohesion into segmentary structures, to fill the political vacuum left by the Turkish administration, and to face the ferocious destructiveness of the French army.

Ultimately, however, Abd al-Kader was defeated and with him went the small residue of a national political tradition that, if it had been permitted to survive, could have acted as the necessary historical link that Algeria's future elite could have used to organize and buttress their sense of national identity. Instead, modern Algeria emerged after 130 years of French colonial rule without an independent political past or tradition, vulnerable and inexperienced.

For all practical purposes, during the second nationalist phase, between 1870 and 1920—that is from the end of the last Kabyle revolt to the immediate post–World War I period —Algerian political and nationalist life was virtually non-existent. Physically reduced, devoid of any remaining and viable indigenous political institutions, and lacking a meaningful traditional urban elite class, Algeria was unable to act during this period. Added to this was the suppression of all protest action.

In 1920, a faint nationalist appeal was first heard in terms of "equal status" enunciated by Algerians seeking equality of rights and the removal of special administrative powers over Muslims. But it was not until the 1920s and 1930s that four separate and identifiable centers of national-ism and opposition made their appearance representing, simultaneously rather than sequentially, the assimilationist, traditionalist, and populist nationalist orientations that had also been articulated by elites in Tunisia and Morocco.

1. The first group consisted of Ferhat Abbas and other Muslim representatives who formed an association of Alger-ian deputies (the Federation of Elected Officials) to foster political, legal, social, and economic assimilation. Its members came primarily from the liberal professions and represented the social or educated elite. The integrationist hopes of these men were dashed by the defeat of the Blum-Violette reform

bill for limited assimilation just before World War II. Assimilationist nationalism proved clearly to be inadequate and all subsequent attempts at reform within the legal French framework failed.

2. Another group of teachers and students of the free schools and their religious mentors combined in 1931 to form an association of the *ulama* to proclaim a religious reformist nationalism that undercut the collaborationist folk religious sects. This nationalitarian-scripturalist orientation limited itself to the defense of cultural identity as represented in the slogan of its *alem* (singular of *ulama*) Ben Badis, "Islam is our religion, Arabic our language, and Algeria our country." Although this group was motivated by pious aims, their objectives—religious freedom, return of confiscated *habous* lands, and the installation of Arabic as the national language —had political implications. Ben Badis rejected assimilation into an alien French culture and proclaimed that Islam was a total social system applicable to Algerian society.

3. The radical populist orientation originated in Paris, not Algeria, as North African workers (mostly Kabyle) and other emigrants to France fell under the spell of the volatile street orator and charismatic nationalist leader, Hajj Messali. He founded in Paris the first Algerian nationalist newspaper. In 1927, he organized the North African Star and when it was banned in 1937, the Algerian People's Party (PPA). He called for total independence, the recall of French troops, the establishment of a revolutionary government, large-scale reforms in land ownership, and the nationalization of industrial enterprises. Messali's call for socialism, a renascent Islam, and Maghrib unity were far ahead of the goals of the other organizations and groups and totally irreconcilable with any current possibilities. As a result, Messali's followers were frustrated and grew increasingly desperate. Yet thanks to its populist methods and the courage of its militants, the PPA laid the foundation for modern nationalism in Algeria.

4. The communists constituted another group who formed

a federation in Algeria in 1924. It was not until 1935, however, that a formal Algerian Communist Party was born. Europeans tended to predominate in this fourth nationalist group and, in any case, no real sense of class consciousness was evident among Algerian workers, thus significantly reducing the political role of the communists in the preindependence nationalist struggle.

The contrasting personalities and political predispositions of such men as Ferhat Abbas, Ben Badis, and Hajj Messali reflected the competing and fragmentary nature of Algerian nationalist aspirations on the eve of World War II.

During the Second World War, nationalist stirrings again began to be felt, this time with greater stridency. The assimilationist approach of Ferhat Abbas, for example, was now abandoned for the idea of a Franco-Algerian community as reflected in his "Manifesto of the Algerian People" issued in 1943 in which he called for the termination of colonialism, the right of Algerians to manage their own affairs, and the implementation of immediate reforms, including the introduction of Arabic as an official language.

Certain token French concessions to Algerian nationalist demands failed to pacify a common opposition held by Abbas, the *ulama,* and Messali's PPA.

All possibility of an evolutionary settlement was destroyed by blunders of postwar French policy and the opposition of the French settlers to any concessions to Muslim aspirations. The ruthless suppression of the riots at Sétif in May 1945, which claimed the lives of some 15,000 Muslims, and the subsequent arrest of Abbas drove many of the nationalist leaders to regard force as the only means of gaining their objective.

Attempts at achieving a political compromise were not totally abandoned, however, as reflected in the founding of a new party by Abbas called the *Union Démocratique du Manifeste Algérien* (UDMA) in 1946. Its call for the creation of an autonomous Algerian republic within the French Union, however, was turned down, further compromising the accommodationist point of view.

From 1948 until the outbreak of the revolution in November 1954, there was little substantial political activity taking place. For many angry young nationalists and incipient radical elites who had tired of temporizing, the UDMA and Abbas were irrelevant and the MTLD (Movement for the Triumph of Democratic Liberties), Messali's succesor to the PPA, was viewed as a single-man authoritarian organization and therefore less germane to broader nationalist needs.

When political means seemed ineffective, Algerian nationalists, impressed by the successful use of force and violence in Tunisia and Morocco, eventually turned to extreme means themselves. Out of this milieu emerged the Revolutionary Committee for Unity and Action (CRUA) which was made up of dissidents from the MTLD, former French army men who had gained valuable experience in the Indochinese campaigns, and miscellaneous groups of dedicated and desperate men who were unafraid of, indeed invited, violence and dangerous risks. The nine "historic chiefs" who in early 1954 had formed the CRUA shared four basic experiences: all of them were radical militants of peasant and working class background, former French army soldiers, members of the *Organisation Spéciale* (OS) that had been founded in the late 1940s by Ahmad Ben Bella and Hocine Ait Ahmed, and all had served time in French prisons.

After several months of preparation during the summer of 1954 in which the military organization was established and the country divided into six *wilayas* or districts, the National Liberation Front (FLN) with its National Liberation Army (ALN) issued a proclamation on November 1, 1954, calling on all Algerians to rise and fight for their freedom. The revolution had begun. In September 1958, the FLN constituted itself into a government, the Provisional

Government of the Algerian Republic (GPRA) which negotiated independence after 1958. A final accord on a cease-
fire was reached at Evian, France, on March 19, 1962, and
formal independence declared on July 3, 1962.

Independence was achieved despite the military impotence
of the revolutionaries and the serious internal divisions existing
within the FLN caused basically by the fact that there had
been neither an incontestable leader, a political organization,
nor an articulated ideology before the revolution. Yet although
the country lay exhausted from the punishing ordeal of a
bloody, indeed savage, eight-year guerrilla war, and the structure of state and society was virtually decimated by the hasty
retreat of frightened colonists, Algeria finally emerged free
and in control over its own political destiny for the first time
in 130 years.

MOROCCO

POSTINDEPENDENCE POLITICS

A T INDEPENDENCE MOROCCO enjoyed a sufficient level of national unity, institutional stability, and effective political leadership that its future viability and growth in the difficult postindependence period of state-building appeared moderately promising. The political parties, with the Istiqlal in the dominant position, provided the necessary cadres for the new government, the urban resistance was incorporated into the police, and the members of the Army of Liberation, who were the last to recognize the monarchy's independence, were absorbed into the Royal Moroccan Army (FAR) or otherwise given positions in the local administration. Other civil servants were recruited from among former employees of the ministries under the protectorate or from newly trained Moroccan youth. Over this political-administrative mosaic representing groups and individuals of widely divergent background and political orientation, King Mohammed V ruled as an apolitical arbitrator and a symbol of Moroccan unity.

On the surface at least it appeared that political life in Morocco might move toward a European model of constitutional democracy based on a competitive multiparty system. Political freedom, while circumscribed, was nonetheless real and utilized. Yet within five years after independence, both the national and political unity that had existed during the period of the colonialist struggle and which had continued immediately after independence and the incipient emergence of quasidemocratic politics virtually disappeared. The formula of sharing power between the king and the Istiqlal and other nationalist leaders soon broke down inasmuch as Mohammed V was unwilling to see his monarchical role reduced to that of a constitutional figurehead and the Istiqlal leadership was unwilling to accept a passive role that the king envisioned for it.

Not only did the Istiqlal never possess full power, but it was also beginning to show signs of internal strain which hampered its attempts to reduce the political dominance of the monarch. Tension between the conservative and radical wings of the party reached a breaking-point in 1959 when Prime Minister Abdullah Ibrahim of the Istiqlal joined a group of young secular-minded intellectuals and trade union leaders to form a new left-wing party called the National Union of Popular Forces (*Union Nationale des Forces Populaires* or UNFP). The UNFP charged the more traditionally minded leadership elements of the Istiqlal with undue caution, compliance with the dictates of the royal household, and indifference to meaningful social reform. Moreover, the new party called for more active government direction of social and economic changes and election of a popular assembly to write a democratic monarchical constitution. In its pursuit of social and economic goals, the UNFP worked closely with the large Moroccan Labor Union (*Union Marocaine du Travail* or UMT).

This split in the country's major independent party organization, which took place formally on January 25, 1959, although the UNFP was not created until September of that same year, signalled the disintegration of the nationalist elite into component groups. This scission can be attributed more to an internally generated process of spontaneous segmentation in the Istiqlal than to the machinations of palace politics which affected the outcome only marginally. In any case, the coming apart of the Istiqlal enabled the palace to manipulate the diverse factions that emerged in the aftermath and explains in great part the king's current control of the political elite. In fact, more than any other political event, the breakup of the Istiqlal has determined the course of politics in independent Morocco.

In the meantime, the king had been developing the institution of the monarchy. His son Hassan, for example, was made acting head of state whenever the king was out of the country. In 1957 Mohammed V officially designated the crown prince as his successor, thus establishing the principle of primogeniture later formally institutionalized in the 1962 constitution. The power of the throne was further consolidated when the police and army, under the direct control of the king, intimidated, harassed, and generally repressed the political activities of an increasingly vocal and oppositional UNFP. Finally, a turning point in the evolution of the monarchy was reached in May 1960, when the king, impatient with the partisanship of party politics and resentful of the increasing criticisms being leveled at monarchical institutions, dismissed the government of Abdullah Ibrahim and his cabinet of predominantly UNFP ministers and appointed himself prime minister with the crown prince as his deputy. For all practical purposes the heir apparent was given effective executive power and with it the beginning of a continuous process of direct monarchical involvement in partisan politics was sent into motion.

On February 25, 1961, King Mohammed V died after routine surgery, and on March 3 Hassan II ascended to the throne. French-educated with a law degree from Bordeaux and thoroughly westernized, Hassan II pursued a policy of consolidating power in his own hands and reducing the political role of the existing parties. Unlike his father, however, the young king lacked charismatic appeal and the advantage of being a nationalist hero. In the absence of genuine popular appeal and devoid of personal standing, Hassan's attempts to strengthen and consolidate the grip of the monarch over national affairs led to serious political schisms at the very top of national power.

The new king's first government, chosen in June 1961, was made up essentially of individuals who were personally loyal to the king rather than representative of any particular program or policy. This was consistent with the king's conception of the role of political parties in the state which was one of organizing supplementary support for the monarchy rather than as an autonomous structure or popular association, designed to formulate policy and programs.

With a minimum of consultation but in keeping with his father's public promise, King Hassan introduced a constitution which was approved in a national referendum on December 7, 1962. Largely inspired by DeGaulle's Fifth Republic, this new national document formally established a constitutional monarchy with guaranteed personal and political freedoms. Yet the constitution's principal provisions worked to further solidify the king's own power at the expense of theoretically representative and freely elected legislative organs. For example, ministers were individually responsible to the king and collectively responsible to a popularly elected house of representatives. In addition, both the legislative jurisdiction of Parliament and the lower house's right to censure the government were severely limited. Moreover, there was provision for an indirectly elected chamber of councillors. Finally, the king was granted the right of dissolution and the right to submit legislation to referenda or further readings, all of which, of course, constituted additional limits to the powers of the lower house. Should all else fail, the king was granted, in Article 35, unlimited emergency powers under conditions where constitutional institutions were in danger of impairment or dissolution.

The first national elections under the 1962 constitution were held in May 1963. In order to organize a popular base of support for himself, Hassan encouraged the creation of parties unquestionably loyal to the throne, namely the Front for the Defense of Constitutional Institutions (*Front pour la Défense des Institutions Constitutionelles* or FDIC) and the conservative Berber party, the Popular Movement (*Mouvement Populaire* or MP). The FDIC sought to mobilize parties and men who had participated in the nationalist movement outside—even in opposition to—the Istiqlal and who would support the monarchy for its own sake or to gain advantage over the Istiqlal.

By all accounts the FDIC was a weak and hastily formed coalition and was unable to project a truly nationalist image. The election, by universal direct suffrage, failed to produce the expected clear majority for the government party with the FDIC winning only 69 of the 144 seats, which was a plurality but not a majority that the king believed his party would receive as confirmation of his authority to rule. The Istiqlal won forty-one seats, the UNFP twenty-eight, and Independents six. In essence, the palace lost the elections of 1963 without the opposition parties winning them.

In the following months, repressive action was taken against both opposition parties. Several Istiqlal deputies were arrested for protesting against corruption and mismanagement of the election, leading the party to boycott further elections later in the year. Almost all leaders of the UNFP were arrested in July 1963, including twenty-one parliamentary representatives in connection with an alleged coup attempt. Many of them were held in solitary confinement, tortured, and eventually sentenced to death.

In this atmosphere the king was unable to command a loyal and effective government as a series of cabinets rose and fell, none commanding strong parliamentary support, for the following two years. The FDIC itself underwent an internal split, further diminishing the king's political standing. Finally, on June 7, 1965, following a series of demonstrations, strikes, and bloody riots by students and workers in Casablanca, Fez, and Rabat, Hassan invoked his constitutional prerogative under article 35, proclaimed a "state of exception," recessed parliament indefinitely, dismissed the prime minister, suspended the constitution, and personally assumed full legislative and executive power.

These actions however, failed to halt the process of political and social unrest that had been sent into motion since the death of Mohammed V. The disappearance and assumed assassination of the popular UNFP leader Mehdi Ben Barka in Paris in October 1965, by agents of the Moroccan government further accelerated the split between the throne and independent political forces in the country. Other disturbances in Morocco followed, including union demonstrations and workers strikes following the 1967 arrest of Mahjoub Ben Siddiq, the popular leader of the UMT, for his criticism of government policy. In 1968, forty-three other UMT leaders were arrested by the government and further unrest ensued. Periodic student strikes, police seizures of newspapers, and mass arrests followed. In fact, the five-year period 1965–1970 witnessed the virtual disappearance of independent political life in Morocco. With the atmosphere already poisoned by rumors of conspiracy and by arrests of hundreds of political opponents and officers, King Hassan continued to rule by executive fiat, constantly shuffling his ministers and keeping the opposition at bay. Although confronted by constant and often violent opposition, the king was determined to rule directly and personally, independent of parties or any formal representative institutions. Denied any real patronage, the opposition parties themselves became less and less able to influence or effect public policies.

When many Moroccans were beginning to fatalistically accept the permanency of the "temporary" suspension of independent constitutional life, it was announced in early July 1970, that a new constitution would be offered for the people's approval in a national referendum later that month. While no single event precipitated the return to constitutional government, it had become increasingly apparent that the monarchy, relying solely on the security forces and the army for unconditional support, had isolated itself and even jeopardized its popularity among the normally supportive mass public. Thus by taking advantage of a period of relative calm, the king hoped to open a new era of cooperation with political parties by reestablishing constitutional authority.

A national referendum on the new constitution was held on July 31, 1970. Despite general opposition from the main political parties, trade unions, and major student organizations, the official figures claimed by the government indicated that over 98 percent of the votes were affirmative. This new constitution represented a significant increase of royal authority over the 1962 constitution which it superceded.

Immediately thereafter, in August 1970, elections for a new single-chamber legislature were held with the Istiqlal and UNFP joining together to form a national front (*kutla wataniya*) first in opposing the ratification of the new constitution and later in boycotting the parliamentary elections. In both instances, however, the *kutla*'s efforts were fruitless, as they were unable to prevent the virtual orchestration of "popular" support for the constitution and new parliament. Of the the 240 members, 90 were elected by direct suffrage, 90 by local councils, and 60 by an electoral college. The results were that 158 elected members were Independents— political nonentities often hand picked by the government for their reliability—60 were of the *Mouvement Populaire,* the only political party to have come out in support of the constitutional referendum, and 22 were from opposition parties. Given the *kutla*'s boycott of the elections and blatant government intervention in the electoral process, including intimidation, vote rigging, and imposing arbitrary and excessive conditions for registration, the apparently overwhelming government victory proved meaningless. If anything, the referendum and elections left the general public and opposition parties in an apathetic and cynical mood. None of these so-called changes in institutional life, however, had an impact on the basic governance of the country which continued to be the prerogative of the court in alliance with a motley array of loyal "independent" politicians, a pervasive system of internal police security, and, always looming in the background, a presumably loyal corps of army officers.

Yet these orchestrated attempts at power balancing and elimination of opposition—the basic components of the elite political culture and the monarchy's basis of retaining tactical superiority over its opponents, both of which will be discussed later—failed to prevent two consecutive attempts, exactly one year apart (July 1971, and August 1972), by disloyal army and air force officers to assassinate the king. Hassan emerged unharmed in both cases but no less determined to suppress, ruthlessly in some cases, the elements which he perceived as intrinsically dangerous. In a series of trials in 1973 and 1974, the authorities handed down death sentences and imprisonments in connection with guerrilla operations in the countryside supposedly masterminded by the UNFP leaders with the support of Colonel Qaddafi of Libya. (Death sentences had previously been handed down following the unsuccessful assassination attempts in 1971 and 1972.) The UNFP itself was officially banned in March 1973.

In between assassination attempts, during the spring of 1972, the king was apparently engaged in reconstructing the political order as he announced a third "new" constitution under which executive power would be vested in the government and the assembly, with two-thirds of the latter's membership being elected by universal suffrage as compared to half under the 1970 constitution. The National Front, caught unprepared by the rapid initiative taken by the king to reassert his political authority in the aftermath of the July 1971 coup attempt, urged a boycott of the constitutional referendum. Specifically, the front condemned the way the constitution was drawn up—unilaterally by the king, as usual—and attacked the government for reducing the real problems of the country to a simple question of constitution referendum. In addition, the parties objected to the king's retention of his power to name the entire government rater than just the premier, of his right to dissolve the chamber, and of his right to rule alone by decree in an emergency. The *kutla* accused the government of rigging the election results, according to which 93 percent of eligible voters took part and approved the constitution in 98.75 percent of valid votes cast. The new constitution was officially promulgated in March 1972, and in April a new cabinet, substantially similar to its predecessor, was appointed to organize elections. On April 30, however, the king announced that Parliament would remain dissolved and that elections for a new assembly were being postponed. No wonder, therefore, that in conjunction with widespread charges of political corruption at the highest levels of government and the continued paralysis of constitutional life, another extralegal attempt to overturn authority, once more unsuccessful, was made in August 1972.

Once again, in the now familiar cycle of repression, violence, and liberalization, the king approached the opposition parties asking for their cooperation in supervising general elections and collaborating with the government. Reflecting as much internal indecision as policy choice, the Istiqlal and UNFP again refused to participate in government unless far-reaching reforms, including curtailing some of the king's powers and guaranteeing political freedom, were instituted. These were unacceptable to the king, who then postponed indefinitely elections that were scheduled to take place in October. In November the king formed a new cabinet, again without opposition participation.

Once the king felt confident that the military had again been brought under his control, he did not hesitate to ignore the demands of the opposition parties who were themselves in political disarray. By the spring of 1972, in fact, the old divergences between the Istiqlal and the UNFP gradually reemerged, virtually eliminating the *kutla*'s already loose coalition in the process. Moreover, within the UNFP itself tactical and ideological differences that had earlier divided the Ibrahim-Ben Siddiq (Casablanca) and Abderrahim Bouabid (Rabat) wings of the UNFP finally led to a formal rupture in July 1972, with the latter reconstituting itself as the Socialist Union of Popular Forces (*Union Socialiste des Forces Populaires* or USFP), while the Casablanca group retained its old name.

All these developments assisted the king in his efforts to retain authority while continuing to sustain his role as "patrimonial arbiter" within Morocco's pluralistic social order. In a manner that has become characterstic of this remarkable monarch, Hassan has combined his skills at manipulating and outmaneuvering the often squabbling opposition parties with liberalization measures which give the impression of change and progress, the combination of which have helped him monopolize power during his eighteen turbulent years as ruler. During 1973, for example, the ever-resourceful monarch responded to his increasing sense of isolation that had resulted from the refusal of opposition parties to participate in government, rural and urban unrest, and military disloyalty and direct attack, by announcing a variety of programs and policies that would regain the political initiative for the throne. In March and May of 1973, the king announced plans for the "Moroccanization" of parts of the economy over the next two years. He also brought out a new and very ambitious Five Year Plan (1973–1977) which called for an average growth ratio of 7.5 percent and more than double the total investment of the previous plan. At the same time he reinforced his traditional support in the rural areas by ordering the confiscation of foreign-owned (mostly French) lands and their distribution among the peasantry.

The king also undertook several foreign policy measures, both substantive and symbolic, that had primarily domestic rather than international objectives. In fact, Hassan has often used the preoccupation with external conflict as a means of defusing domestic unrest and mobilizing the population under the banner of national unity. In its relations with Spain, for example, the crown assumed a nationalist stand by extending Moroccan jurisdiction over coastal waters from twelve to seventy miles, thereby cutting into the highly profitable Spanish sardine and tuna fishing business. Only protracted negotiations resulting in a formal agreement between the two countries in January 1974, prevented a possible conflict. Yet the king derived significant domestic "mileage" from his strong stand. Likewise, Moroccan troops were dispatched to the Syrian and Egyptian fronts during the October 1973 Arab-Israeli war, further enhancing the king's image as a supporter of Palestine and Arab nationailst causes, the "sacred cows" of mass politics in the Arab world.

Even during the early months of 1974, when political trials and further arrests were taking place, Hassen made several conciliatory gestures which enhanced his prestige among the people. In March 1974, for example, he announced plans for university and judicial reforms, and in April several imprisoned UNFP leaders were released. He also gained considerable popular support with his strong nationalist stand on the question of Spanish Sahara, the northern two-thirds of which he hoped to annex directly to Morocco. In July 1974, the king held consultations with military leaders, ministers, and leaders of all the political parties in preparation for a vigorous diplomatic and, if need be, military effort on the Sahara question. With the resolution of the Sahara problem in Morocco's favor, achieved with virtually no bloodshed and little cost, the monarchy once again felt politically secure.

The crown's stature was also bolstered economically by

the 350 percent rise in world phosphate prices—Morocco is the world's leading exporter of phosphates—in little more than a year (from U.S. $14 a ton in December 1973, to $63 in January 1975). Yet with all these apparent signs of new political vitality and economic vigor, the king gave no indication that he intended to relinquish any of his political powers or monarchical privileges, although he kept alive the hope of some future legislative elections. After several postponements and delays such elections finally did take place on June 3, 1977, marking a kind of return to parliamentary democracy after nearly seven years of virtual political dictatorship.

In a manner reminiscent of all previous such "democratic" endeavors, the monarchy scored a landslide victory over the opposition and leftist groupings. The independents, who described themselves as "unconditionally monarchist," won 81 of the 176 seats contested for the new chamber of representatives. To this was added the total of thirty-three seats won by the three right-wing parties who declared their intention of working with the independents thereby assuring the monarchy of a large and comfortable majority. Among independents elected, often with sizable majorities, were Prime Minister Ahmed Osman, the king's brother-in-law, and fourteen other members of the present (June 1977) government.

The Istiqlal made somewhat of a surprise showing, winning a respectable fourty-five seats and reaffirming, in the process, its potential for organizational and electoral strength. The same could not be said of the radical USFP which suffered a humiliating defeat gaining only sixteen seats in the new chamber. Even the party's popular leader, Abderrahim Bouabid, was unsuccessful in his bid for a parliamentary seat.

On the surface at least, it would appear that the king has regained the political initiative, reconstructed the security forces in a manner supportive of the crown, and established his political as well as legislative constitutional dominance over the left-wing opposition. He has also taken several important and symbolically successful foreign policy initiatives, including resolving the Sahara question in Morocco's favor, taking a more vigorous "Arabist" position on the Arab-Israeli conflict, and making an impressive showing in the Zaire conflagration of April 1977, in which approximately fifteen hundred elite Moroccan troops were sent to assist President Mobutu to put down an attack by secessionist Katanga forces stationed in neighboring Angola. All of this has combined to enhance the King's prestige and given further popular support to the institution of the monarchy.

Yet persistent and profound social, economic, and political problems remain that give serious doubt to the durability of Hassan's current "successes" and the viability of resurrected constitutional life. For example, corruption has spread throughout the society, and nepotism, favoratism, and old-fashioned *bakshish* (bribery) have become increasingly institutionalized in the central administration, notwithstanding Hassan's occasional campaigns against corruption within the government including jailing a number of former high officials. The military, although now in check, remains unpredictable and therefore a threat to state and society. The party system remains moribund as it becomes more and more difficult to recruit young and capable members. Political apathy runs deep as the futility of participation becomes more evident. Moroccan youth have become increasingly alienated from the regime. Likewise, the labor unions have been politically neutralized. But probably the most serious threat to the monarchical system of rule lies in the ineffective economic system that is unable to bridge the ever-increasing gap between the wealthy few and the impoverished many. In fact, Morocco is today in danger of being split apart into an ever-smaller, ever-richer elite, and an ever-growing and, by comparison, ever-poorer mass of the people. This inequitable distribution of wealth, where 10 percent of the population absorbs 45 percent of the nation's wealth, will remain in the near and intermediate future King Hassan's most pressing and politically most explosive problem.

POLITICAL CULTURE

The concept of political culture seeks to analyze the orientations and psychological predispositions of a population towards political life. For any society political culture involves the linking of those dimensions of an individual's thoughts, feelings, or behaviors to the creation and maintenance of a society's fundamental political order. Moreover, political culture provides an explanation of how such sentiments influence political action—the ways in which the people respond to authority, the political roles they play, and their degree of participation in political affairs. In other words, political culture guides the behavior of political actors and contains the catalysts as well as the constraints to political action. Regardless of ideological orientation or political intent, most regimes are captives of their own political culture.

One of the most outstanding features of North African political culture is the pervasiveness and intensity of political distrust manifest among all politicians. All too frequently political disputes degenerate into personal vendettas. The very notion of power is conceived by Maghribi politicians as a coercive instrument rather than as a cooperative process. Such attitudes toward power may have been understandable in the precolonial period when the sphere of politics was limited, authority was distant, and distrust ameliorated by the ideal of piety and the personal consultations of the benign Islamic ruler. The forced imposition of modern, impersonal administration, however, reinforced the native distrust of authority while radically expanding the scope of power and politics. The colonialist repression of Maghribi nationalist movements made the development of a cooperative conception of power even more difficult to achieve. If anything, it served to substitute conspiratorial action and clandestine behavior for legitimate political discourse.

Nowhere is conspiratorial politics more evident than in postindependence Morocco where political distrust and tension are nearly universal. The system lacks agreed-upon "rules of the game" by which decisions are cooperatively made. Instead, Moroccan political life is forever in a state of heightened political tension which rarely, however, spills over into open conflict. What keeps the system intact is the overriding desire of its elite members and political participants to defend their positions in a system of equilibrium, neither destroying their rivals nor seeking to initiate any great movement of change. In fact, the preoccupation with defense reveals a basic characteristic of Moroccan political behavior: the outstanding flexibility and maneuverability of political actors and groups.

In a defensively oriented political universe, the politician is forever prepared to enter into all sorts of improbable alliances and unlikely associations. Inevitably, such a process leads to political stalemate or decay which is another salient feature of present-day Moroccan politics. And this stalemate, in turn, is based upon the notion of "segmental opposition" as derived from the maintenance of tribal structure. Now, however, the tensions and conflicts that historically kept "segments" of the tribe in a sort of functional equilibrium have been transferred to contemporary Moroccan social groups whose behavior very much resembles that of traditional segmentary tribal systems.

The group orientation has always existed in Morocco and continues to play an important part in the political culture and behavior of the country. Most individuals, for example, have difficulty perceiving themselves or others as independent actors removed from the familiarity and guidance of the group. In fact, it is only in relationship to the group that a Moroccan identifies himself. Most importantly, it is only in the context of the group that a man achieves security.

It is within this group framework that one can best understand the almost continuous process of alliance-building and alliance-maintenance that so involves Moroccan elites and nonelites alike. Since he believes that everyone else is involved in this alliance-formation process, the Moroccan must be alert to those that might out-maneuver or trick him. As a leading scholar of Moroccan politics has observed: "Covert machinations, dissimulation, and trickery are accepted as the facts of political life, and a man's ostensible motives for a given action cannot be trusted. In his dealings with others, and this is true on a national and international scale, the Moroccan takes for granted an element of conspiracy." [Waterbury, 1970:77]

The peculiar irony of this system of segmentary cleavages with its high degree of tension and incipient conflict is that it has led to increased group cohesion rather than group disintegration. This cohesion, however, remains based on a negative consensus in which segmentation is combined with narrow, shared interests rather than upon an overarching political or nationalist ideology. In fact, given the defensive preoccupation with survival and the conspiratorial character of Moroccan political culture and behavior, the emergence and maintenance of a credible ideology seems highly unlikely. Except for political belief systems predicated upon Islamic fundamentalist principles, which still find meaning among many of the tradition-bound masses, it seems doubtful that a broadly based nationalist ideology can take hold in such a fluid milieu. *Civisme,* for example, a blend of civic spirit and religious values, through which Hassan has hoped to influence future citizens and subjects, has simply failed to capture the imagination and interests of its targeted audiences, particularly the youth. Moreover, the numerous groups and alliances that dominate the intricate and complex web of Moroccan politics are themselves virtually devoid of any political or programmatic coloration; for these groups there is no commitment to a political program but simply short-term tactical objectives. It is thus almost meaningless to talk about political ideology in Morocco today, however much ideological sloganeering and rhetorical posturing may take place among the relatively small group of alienated intellectuals, dissident university students, and disaffected oppositional politicos.

POLITICAL STRUCTURES

Morocco's political structures and institutions are only vaguely congruent with the country's political culture and style of political discourse. Although constitutional life was formally introduced in 1962, only about six years (1962–1965, 1970–1971, and post-June 1977) since that time has national politics been conducted within the framework of a constitution. On ascending the throne on March 3, 1961, King Hassan II declared his support for the royal charter proclaimed by his father, Mohammed V, in 1958. This charter outlined steps toward establishing a constitutional monarchy. A constitution providing for representative government under a strong monarchy was approved by referendum in December 1962, and elections were held in May 1963. In June 1965, following the bloody student riots and civil unrest described earlier, the constitution was suspended when the king declared a "state of exception" under Article 35 of the constitution and assumed full legislative as well as executive and regulatory powers.

After five years of virtual one-man rule, King Hassan submitted to referendum a new constitution in July 1970. Its approval and subsequent elections formally ended the 1965 "state of exception." It collapsed, however, with the attempted military coup d'état of July 10, 1971. A third constitution was introduced in March 1972, and approved by popular referendum. Its implementation was shortcircuited by a second coup attempt on August 16, 1972. Although repeated promises of national elections under the 1972 constitution were made by the king, it was not until five years after the second abortive coup that such elections finally did take place. Preceded by a series of local and provincial elections begun on November 12, 1976, national elections took place on June 3, 1977, when two-thirds of the 264-member unicameral legislature was elected by direct universal suffrage. Nearly three weeks later the other third of the parliament was elected by an electoral college composed of councillors in local government and employers' and employees' representatives. On the surface at least, constitutional democracy has been revived in Morocco.

According to the provisions of the 1972 constitution, Morocco is described as a constitutional, democratic, and social monarchy with Islam as the official state religion. The constitution provides for equality before the law and guarantees freedom of movement, speech, opinion, and assembly. Amendments to the constitution may be initiated by either the king or the legislature, but such initiatives require approval in a popular referendum.

The power and authority of the monarchy are expansive with political power highly centralized in the hands of the king. The king is the supreme civil and religious authority in the state, the latter as "Commander of the Faithful," and the commander-in-chief of the armed forces. The crown is hereditary and usually transmitted to the eldest son, but another son may be designated should the king so desire. The king appoints all important officials, including the premier and the cabinet. He promulgates legislation passed by the legislature. He has the authority to dissolve the legislature, to declare a state of emergency during which he may rule by decree (under Article 35, which was invoked in 1965), and to sign and ratify treaties. He presides over the cabinet, the Council for National Development and Planning, and the Supreme Judicial Council.

Although the constitution attributes sovereignty to the nation which exercises it directly by referendum and indirectly through constitutional institutions, the powers given to the king have been far more important than the so-called sovereignty of the nation. The whole manner in which government is conducted has shifted power away from the elected representatives and party leaders and concentrated it in the monarchy. Legal stipulations and constitutional provisions simply reinforce the all-pervasive authoritarian rule of the king.

The 1972 constitution vests legislative authority in a unicameral house of representatives elected for a four-year term. Among the legislature's constitutional powers include the right to initiate constitutional amendments, authorize declarations of war, and approve extensions of a state of emergency beyond thirty days. The king may request the legislature to reconsider legislation before giving his assent, submit proposed legislation to a referendum, and dissolve parliament if a referendum rejects a proposed law. He may also dissolve the house by decree and call for new elections, but he cannot dissolve the succeeding house for a year.

The Moroccan judicial and administrative systems reflect both French and Spanish influences. The country is administratively divided into nineteen provinces and two urban prefectures, Casablanca and Rabat. The provinces are further divided into seventy-two administrative areas and communes. Each of the administrative regions is headed by a governor, appointed by the king and responsible to him. On April 12, 1976, the king appointed governors to three administrative provinces in Morocco's sector of the former Spanish Sahara.

The judicial system is headed by a supreme court (*Majlis al-A'ala*), composed of four chambers: civil, criminal, administrative and social. The *Majlis* supervises an ordinary court system consisting of three courts of appeal, each of which, in turn, oversees lower regional tribunals. There are fourteen labor tribunals to settle management-labor disputes and labor contract disputes. In 1965, a special court to deal with corruption among public officials was established. All judges are appointed by the king with the advice of the Supreme Judicial Council. Moroccan courts administer a system based on Islamic law but strongly influenced by the French and Spanish legal systems.

Morocco's constitutional system, like that of her neighbors to the east, provides only a glimpse at the actual configuration of power in the state. In fact, despite real differences in social structure and national policy, the three political systems of the Maghrib display remarkable similarities with respect to the power structure. Notwithstanding the variations in constitutional wording and personal style, Morocco's King Hassan II, the late Houari Boumediene of Algeria and his successor, Chadli Benjedid, and Tunisia's Habib Bourguiba all exercise broadly comparable, comprehensive powers in the absence of any effective political opposition. Each leader has to date successfully consolidated power by playing-off competing groups and rival factions and, if need be, eliminating them altogether as threats to his personal power as the cases of Mehdi Ben Barka of Morocco, Salah Ben Youssef of Tunisia, and Belkacem Krim of Algeria so well demonstrate (all of whom were "mysteriously" assassinated in Europe). While systems of consultation and advice prevail within the broader power structures, including constitutional ones, no formal, systematic procedures force the ruler to implement proffered advice.

POLITICAL PROCESSES

Moroccan political processes are dominated by a group of approximately one thousand men who constitute the country's political elite. Leaders of the various political parties and other formal and informal groups and associations, including chief representatives of labor unions, economic organizations, and agricultural interests speak for and control most of those who are politically active and who hold specific political attitudes. Among all these political parties, pressure groups, and regional interests a fierce competition for power and patronage takes place. Although an apparent political pluralism seems to prevail, in fact political life is monopolized by those qualities inherent to the monarch's personal charisma or *baraka*. Regardless of what the more modernized sectors of society may personally think of the monarch, he is deeply venerated by the rural masses who view the *sharif* (commander) as a dispenser of *baraka*. In short, Islamic tradition remains an important source of legitimacy for the throne.

Beyond the king's traditional position as head of a historic dynasty and as commander of the faithful of the national religion, the monarchy represents the symbolic leadership of the nationalist struggle. In the minds of the masses, national independence and political unification are intimately associated with monarchical authority, however marginal the king's actual political contribution may have been in the preindependence nationalist movement.

The king's power and prestige are further enhanced by the fact that he is the nation's most prominent dispenser of patronage and the ultimate source of spoils in the system. The palace has a very real command over Moroccan commercial activities as well as over the distribution of patronage, both of which it uses to sustain the king's secular clientele and to build his secular alliances. Indeed, these commercial and patronage resources are the king's two most effective levels of elite control.

As we have seen, Moroccan society consists of numerous segments related to one another by tension and conflict. Because this has historically been a constant factor in Moroccan politics, one of the most consistently rewarding political roles in the country has been that of arbiter among conflicting groups. Both Mohammed V and Hassan II have consciously and publicly adopted this crucial arbiter function which, more than anything else, has made the monarch the pivotal center of Morocco's disparate political forces characterized as they are by intense fragmentation and factionalization.

The success of the arbiter function has been based on the operation of two simultaneous processes aimed at insuring the king's political supremacy. On the one hand, the king continues to recognize and encourage the allegiance shown him by the various parties and, on the other, sets about developing ways of strengthening his own sources of support at the expense of the very same parties. Once the parties appear too strong, the king will work to weaken, but not destroy, the support of the parties. His ability to successfully manage such a balance lies in his reaffirming the direct ties between himself and the people and also involves playing the Istiqlal, as the country's predominant organization, off against rival power-seeking parties and political organizations. In this manner the king can then claim the role of honest broker among the groups he had encouraged or disparaged, without being identified with or indebted to any one of them. In this arbiter role, therefore, the monarchy has succeeded in creating and maintaining a sort of circular strategy in which intergroup rivalry is encouraged. Such discontinuous political leadership then highlights the need for a symbol of political continuity, namely the throne.

Beyond the initial arbiter function, a few simple principles have further guided monarchical rule since independence. First, no group may be permitted to become too strong. If, by accident and inadvertently, this should appear to be happening, then rival groups are encouraged to emerge, propped up, or otherwise given new political life to counter such potential hegemonic tendencies of any single group, organization, or individual. At the same time, however, no group or organization should be allowed to die altogether, including the opposition parties. While attrition, feebleness, and quiescence are all tolerated, indeed encouraged, the basic skeletal structure of any organization must ultimately remain if it is to be revived for some future purpose. A final basic rule that the monarchy follows is that of avoiding becoming too closely identified with any single group or its leaders and policies. This has the natural advantage of permitting the king to adjust accordingly to the political fortunes of any group.

When all else fails, power and control can be maintained via the "king's men." An executive staff, the intelligence and security branches of the Ministry of the Interior and the Ministry of National Defense, including a once-again loyal army and officer corps, all assist in the maintenance of royal authority throughout the kingdom.

The past and current success of such a system of royal control has been predicated on the nature of the Moroccan political elite itself. As long as the elite remained small, socially and educationally homogeneous yet politically fragmented and introverted, the throne has maintained the ability to divide it, manipulate it, and use it for its own purposes. Both the size of the elite and the balance of its component parts cannot be guaranteed in the future however, as rapid population and educational growth will inevitably upset this equilibrium at all social levels, including that of the elite. The implications of this long-term demographic process on the monarchy's hegemonic role in the system is well summarized by John Waterbury who writes:

> The post-1956 emphasis on mass education combined with a veritable demographic explosion has pumped unprecedented numbers of Moroccans into all levels of the educational system. Education has been a key to elite status in the past, and it is unlikely that many of these youths will settle for anything less in the future. Moreover, the new aspirants will not have the common social background of the present elite, the nationalist movement means little to them, and it is improbable that existing alliance and obligation systems will be able to absorb more than a small number of them. Either the elite of today will ignore the future aspirants, and will as a result become obsolete, or it will attempt to absorb them and thus will change utterly its behavior, its size, and its nature. [Waterbury, 1970:164]

POLITICAL PARTIES

On paper Morocco resembles a multiparty system. In fact, all three of Morocco's postindependence constitutions have included an article explicitly prohibiting a single-party system. This was originally done as a means of combating the monopoly of the Istiqlal consistent with the monarchy's principle of ruleship discussed above. Yet since the early 1960s and particularly under the reign of Hassan II, the outcome of party competition either at the polls or in parliament has not decisively affected the composition or policies of the king's government. Except for those which may be regarded as semi-officially sponsored by the monarchy, Morocco's political parties have remained largely outside the mainstream of governmental power. The centralized role of the monarchy, the king's tactic of playing off one party against another for the purpose of preventing the crystallization of a political force strong enough to threaten the position of the monarchy, and the pervasive factional infighting and internal party splits have all combined to severely undermine the efficacy of party life notwithstanding the revival of party activity in the recent legislative elections of June 3, 1977.

Next to the monarchy the Istiqlal Party remains the most influential political force in the country; its complex internal divisions faithfully reflect the social forces and psychological tensions of Morocco's pluralist society. Like other Moroccan political forces, however, the Istiqlal shares influence without responsibility. From its inception the largest of Moroccan political organizations, the Istiqlal—which grew out of nationalist movements of the 1930s and was formally organized in 1943—has seen itself as a "school room" for political, social, and cultural education. It was instrumental in achieving Moroccan independence but was unable to maximize its national stature and popularity in the immediate postindependence period. Although considered superior to all other political parties in the way its leadership could apply the principles of organization, communications, and discipline, the Istiqlal was unable to transform itself either before or after independence into an effective mass-based party. Even its status as the nationalist symbol was displaced by the sultan. But probably the root of the party's inadequacy lies in the nature of Moroccan society itself and the natural divisions of its political organizations. The Istiqlal was never a party of individuals joined together according to some sort of consensus on programs or desirable political activities but, instead, remained an agglomeration of groups which had integrated themselves into the party as groups, and with purely defensive objectives in mind. Ultimately, divisions were based more on personal animosities than on basic ideological or programmatic conflicts. In any case, such breaches were pretexts rather than causes for political action, as with the split in early 1959 creating the National Union of Popular Forces.

The Istiqlal represents a traditional, defensive, and status-quo segment of small urban and rural population, with its traditional strongholds in Fez and Meknès. Its founding father and venerable leader was Allal al-Fassi, who died in May 1973. He was replaced by Mohamed Boucetta as secretary-general rather than president of the party.

The Istiqlal subscribes to a form of Islamic socialism hoping to cultivate a radical progressive image. It is firmly attached to the principles of Islam and at the same time expresses a commitment to. economic independence, land reform ("the land to those who work it"), and economic equality. Ideological rhetoric aside, however, the Istiqlal remains the party of landowning and commercial interests. Its conservative leadership undermines its progressive "socialist" platform.

Although originally monarchist, the Istiqlal has been in opposition since the early 1960s. It rarely attacks the king or monarchy directly, however, since it remains eager for office and a share in governmental power. Its relatively impressive performance in the June 1977 elections for the house of representatives has boosted its political standing and reconfirmed its status as the only credible opposition force in the country. However, the extent to which recent electoral victories are translated into concrete political rewards will depend upon the wishes of the king and the pluralist system he manipulates, as has been the case for the last two decades.

The UNFP arose out of the schism between radical and conservative wings of the Istiqlal in 1959, and is today made up of a coalition of left-wing nationalists, trade-unionists, resistance fighters, and dissident members of minor parties.

The party's symbolic hero and political ideologue was Mehdi Ben Barka, an original founder of the splinter group who represented leftist and radical political trends as reflected in his marxist vocabulary and occasionally radical methods. With Ben Barka's disappearance and presumed assassination in 1965, Abdullah Ibrahim assumed the leadership of the party which he still heads today.

Under continuous pressure and harassment by the throne and weakened by serious internal factionalism, the UNFP was never able to achieve much influence or prestige among Moroccans, save the relatively constant support provided it by left-wing trade unions, especially the *Union Marocaine du Travail* (UMT), the country's largest labor federation.

The party's internal divisions came to a head in 1972 when the National Administrative Committee suspended the ten-man secretariat-general and the three-man political bureau and replaced them with a collection of five permanent committees. The political bureau thereupon formed its own organization, UNFF-Rabat section, which was banned for several months in 1973 for activities against the state and subsequently reorganized as the Socialist Union of Popular Forces.

UNFP policies have consistently shown an antimonarchist tendency and its theoreticians subscribe to a marxist ideology. Its radical posture and revolutionary rhetoric has made it attractive to a very narrow yet critical sector of Moroccan urban society including university students and workers. But its status as the foremost radical opposition has been somewhat usurped with the formal creation of the USFP in September 1974.

The UNFP-Rabat section, which had dissociated itself from the Casablanca section in July 1972, was accused by the government of involvement in a Libyan-aided plot to overthrow King Hassan in March 1973. The USFP calls for thorough reform of the nation's social, economic, and administrative structures, nationalization of the principal means of production, and a general amnesty for all political prisoners. Its recent participation in the June 1977 national elections proved disastrous to its political standing as its leader and secretary general, Abderrahim Bouabid, was defeated, and the party managed to obtain a mere 16 seats of the 176 being contested. Hard-liners within the party had pressured against participation in elections which were subsequently described by Bouabid as "rigged and manipulated" by the authorities. More likely, the USFP's ideological extremism and radical intentions intimidated an otherwise conservative electorate which apparently heeded the Istiqlal's warning of the "yellow threat" (the USFP's color) during the electoral campaign.

The Party of Progress and Socialism (*Parti du Progrès et du Socialisme* or PPS) was formed in 1968 to replace the banned Moroccan Communist Party and is headed by its long-time secretary-general, Ali Yata. Although the PPS was itself banned in 1969, it was resurrected in late 1974 and took part in the June 1977 elections in which Ali Yata successfully gained a seat in the new house of representatives. This development placed Morocco in the unique position of having a legitimately elected communist representative in its parliament, the only such case for a monarchy anywhere in the Arab and African worlds.

A number of minor, weakly organized independent and promonarchy parties of dubious political significance, save that of necessary elements in the royal game of divide-and-rule, round out the political party system in Morocco.

Like political immobilism in Morocco as a whole, so too have political parties been unable to establish a credible and effective posture in the country. They simply remain other players in a complex and highly divided social structure. The center of policies continues to be the monarchy with the political organizations remaining as either faithful, indifferent, or disgruntled bystanders.

THE ARMY

For a long time the army (referring to all the armed forces) in Morocco was considered as a loyal apolitical force under the direct control of the king and thus subordinate to civilian rule. When in July 1963, the government uncovered a plot against the internal security of the state, the military was implicated and the army and air force hierarchies were quietly shaken up as a result. Since that alleged plot, the king has developed the military as a pillar of his regime and in the process absolutely forbidden the involvement of military officers in any opposition political movement.

For nearly a decade thereafter, with the financial and technical assistance of the Americans and French, the Royal Moroccan Army (*Forces Armées Royales* or FAR) developed as a relatively modern, well-equipped and effective fighting force which, in combination with the internal security forces, riot police, and secret agents, appeared to insure the monarchy's political and physical security. Earlier FAR had been made the personal responsibility of Prince Hassan who organized and controlled it and, later as king, had final authority in all promotions. In addition, the king always made certain that the material needs of the military were being adequately met.

Yet with all this, no one was prepared for the two successive aborted coups undertaken by the army and air force respectively in July 1971, and August 1972. From the staunchest supporters of the throne, the Moroccan military literally overnight turned into the most serious threat to the monarchy since independence. The myth of the loyalty of the army had been severely tested if not destroyed. King Hassan was quick to reconstruct the security forces and provide them with diversions including direct involvement in the Sahara dispute and the brief foray into Zaire as a means of reestablishing the military's loyalty.

Yet there can never again be certainty that the military will remain indifferent to the profound social dislocations occurring in the society including widespread and government-sanctioned corruption, unemployment, mass rural poverty, student alienation, and a Byzantine political process which may once more lead it to pursue drastic and conclusive action as the only means to effect substantial change. To this must be added the changing social background and educational levels of new army recruits who are less committed to patrimonial attachments and the power of local and national patrons including the king. As guardians of the state's coercive power, the army will remain of incalculable political significance simply because it is there, "semi-unknown, in the back of all civilian minds, a sort of lurking threat . . . forming an inescapable back-drop against which all political decisions are taken." [Waterbury, 1970:84]

STUDENTS

University students in Morocco as elsewhere in the Middle East and North Africa constitute an important force in the country's political life, both as incipient, aspiring elites and as current elements of support or opposition to existing political arrangements. Given the relatively small numbers that achieve university status and that a university degree is a prerequisite for entry into elite-level positions including political ones, the attitudes and behavior of students assume increasing significance.

By far the most active and politically significant element among Moroccan youth has been the university students. At a relatively early age and long before they complete formal studies, students become aware of the importance of politics. The political parties cultivate this interest and organize students in party-affiliated associations.

The National Union of Moroccan Students (*Union Nationale des Etudiants Marocains* or UNEM) is the major Moroccan student union founded in 1956 by Ben Barka then of the Istiqlal. After the split in 1959, UNEM remained closely identified with the National Union of Popular Forces (UNFP), while the Istiqlal organized its own separate student union, the General Union of Moroccan Students (*Union Générale des Etudiants Marocains* or UGEM) which, however, was never able to gain the sympathy or support of very many students.

Since the 1960s, students have been extensively involved in numerous extralegal and intensely oppositional activities directed against the regime and its incumbents, most of whom are viewed with hostility, contempt, or indifference. Whether working through its parent organizations or simply as anomic interest groups, students have demonstrated against a wide range of political, social, economic, and educational grievances usually articulated in the highly ideological language of Arab politics such as Arab socialism, Arab nationalism, revolutionism, imperialism, and neocolonialism. In recent years students have also been affected by an increasing alienation from and disenchantment with political and social life at large as job opportunities after graduation continue to diminish, social injustice and economic inequality become more pronounced, and manipulative palace politics proceed unhampered by any credible political or military opposition. This is why there was such general enthusiasm among students for the 1971 and 1972 attempted coups and, subsequently, such disappointment when they were crushed. Increased student discontent with the existing state of political affairs has led the more radical youth to outflank even the leftist opposition. In early 1972, for example, UNEM, whose executive committee was dominated by radical students, became independent of UNFP.

Since the resentment and hostility of elite aspirants remains diffuse and relatively unorganized, the regime has been able to control the small band of hard-core militants who are, nonetheless, well disciplined, indoctrinated, and dedicated to revolutionary causes. Given the burgeoning birth rate, the majority of youth in the population, the stagnant economy, and the political stalemate evident among the system's status-quo elites, it seems unlikely that students can for long be put off, muzzled, imprisoned, or co-opted to neutralize or eliminate their potential for political unrest. Incomplete socialization, rapid socioeconomic change, the worldwide communications revolution, the rise of and fascination with radical Third World ideologies, and the increasing irrelevance of patrimonial politics all combine to create an atmosphere of instability and potential revolution that is bound to encourage continued student expression of anti-regime sentiments but with increasing militancy and, inevitably, bloodshed.

LABOR UNIONS

The Moroccan trade union movement acquired skill, conviction, and solidarity by having to struggle both against colonial repression and communist control of unions during the decade preceding national independence. After 1956, given much greater freedom to organize and strike, the Union of Moroccan Labor (UMT), established in 1955 by Tayyib Bouazza and Mahjoub Ben Seddiq, swelled its membership to become the largest and strongest trade union in all of the Middle East and North Africa. From its inception the UMT was nationalist, not communist, and allied to the Istiqlal. With the split in the Istiqlal, it went into the UNFP camp and provided its main popular and organized support.

Until 1960, the UMT was Morocco's sole labor and trade

union confederation. In that year the Istiqlal organized a rival union, the General Union of Moroccan Workers (*Union Générale des Travailleurs Marocains* or UGTM). But this has remained a dependent organization unable to compete in size with the UMT. Since then all other Moroccan political parties have followed suit but with meager success. The UMT has remained the largest confederation, commanding the allegiance of the majority of workers, and is by far the best organized.

Despite the UMT's historically significant role both in cooperation with and in opposition to the regime, the general political and economic climate in Morocco remains hostile to the development of a vigorous and independent labor movement. Three particular factors inhibit such development: first, the high level of unemployment makes the unions insecure and vulnerable to sudden, unplanned changes in membership, recruitment, financial support, and organizational solidarity. Second, the unions are subject both to harsh pressure and sweet blandishments from the government. Finally, there exists very serious divergences between trade union interests and those of the politicians. Added to all this, of course, is the constant factor of monarchical interference in which the king utilizes the same instruments of creating and accentuating divisions rather than fostering unity that have so successfully been applied against the opposition political parties.

POLITICAL ECONOMY

The Moroccan strategy of development has concentrated public expenditure on the development of agriculture. Agriculture is the key to the economy of Morocco; nearly 70 percent of the population derive their living directly or indirectly from the soil. Agriculture supplies almost 90 percent of the country's domestic food requirements and almost 50 percent of the country's total merchandise exports. In 1975, agriculture contributed 30 percent to the GNP (Gross National Product).

The plains and uplands of western Morocco between the Atlas ranges and the Atlantic Ocean, together with the intermontane valleys of the Middle Atlas range, constitute the main agricultural region.

Despite the country's congenial climate and varied soils, Morocco's agriculture is confronted with a number of serious problems. Predominant among these is the increasing lack of water as one moves from northwest to southeast and the year-to-year unpredictability of rainfall. This situation is compounded by historical factors in the traditional sector. Primitive methods of cultivation, a lack of understanding of the use of fertilizers and insecticides, and the absence of a means to acquire them contribute to low yields on the vast majority of farms. Fragmentation of land among heirs, resulting from the provisions of traditional Muslim inheritance laws, has created large numbers of minute, irregularly shaped, and often widely scattered plots that are inefficient to cultivate.

The physical situation makes difficult the use of modern equipment in the traditional sector and, together with extreme poverty, continues to tie the Moroccan peasant to the hoes, wooden plows, and pointed sticks used by his ancestors. Frequent droughts and insect plagues make the life of the subsistence farmer even more precarious.

The traditional sector accounts for approximately 85 to 90 percent of the total agricultural area, and a modern sector accounts for the rest. The modern system was introduced by Europeans, primarily French settlers, in the first half of the twentieth century on land taken over by the protectorate government that was to be colonized or purchased from Moroccans by private owners. The modern sector included an estimated 2.5 million acres of agricultural land, most of which was under field or tree crops.

Although the modern sector comprised only about 10 or 15 percent of total agricultural land, it included some of the most fertile land in the country, and it contributed over 85 percent of commercialized agricultural production, including almost all of the citrus fruit, fresh vegetables, wine, soft wheat, and other export crops. Much of the agricultural land in the traditional sector is devoted to grazing, and the average yields per acre of cropped land are less than half those in the modern sector. The traditional sector supports over 1 million families which, even in good years, consume nearly all that they produce.

On balance, the development of Moroccan agriculture since 1956 has been characterized by conservatism, coupled with an emphasis on technical progress, rather than by social change. Despite occasionally imaginative projects and certain active programs of public works, the government has been unable to restructure the duality of the agricultural sector nor overcome the obvious problems of poverty and unemployment in the underendowed agricultural areas.

Mineral resources make an important contribution to the GNP. Morocco's most promising source of overall economic growth is its phosphate industry. In fact, Morocco is the world's largest exporter of phosphates with a 1973 sales of 16 million tons. With a 450 percent boost in prices in 1973–74, phosphates rose to 48 percent of total exports in 1974. Major investments in expansion of production are planned: $524 million under the current five year plan (1973–1977) or 10 percent of the total national investment. With the price increase, unforseen in the original plan, this figure may increase and with it the projected increase of production of 13 percent. This windfall, however, is somewhat offset by the simultaneous sharp increase in oil prices since the country remains essentially oil poor. In addition, the disastrous effects of drought on the country's agriculture in the 1973–75 period has also been costly.

Aside from phosphates, industry plays a minor part in the Moroccan economy, and this is particularly true of manufacturing industry. Yet in this and other areas of the economy, there appears to be a greater governmental determination to produce changes. Official government figures for the 1968–72 period, for example, report that the Gross Domestic Product increased at an average annual rate of 5.7 percent well above the rate of 4.3 percent targeted in the plan for the same period. This rate is targeted to reach 7.5 percent in the current 1973–77 plan.

The present five year plan assumes a significant increase in the role of the state. The public sector contribution of investment is to total $2.8 billion, double that of the previous plan, or 42 percent of the total. In addition, the public sector is to play a leading role in the "Moroccanization" of foreign business. The Moroccanization of industry was introduced in 1973 followed by a new code of investments. The Moroccanization decrees were effectively designed to increase Moroccan participation in share capital and in the direction of private industry by a limited definition of what constituted a Moroccan company (commercial enterprises had to be at least 50 percent Moroccan owned).

Foreign-owned agricultural land was finally expropriated by the state under the same March 1973 Moroccanization decrees, paving the way for the distribution of 400,000 hectares to small farmers and the expansion of a cooperatives program. The political importance of this land distribution has been obvious. The rate of distribution, for example, increased rapidly over the years of the two attempts on the king's life (nineteen thousand hectares in 1971, and more than ninety thousand in 1972). In the same period the king went so far as to make available six thousand hectares of his own land in ceremonies accompanied by colorful celebrations in the countryside.

Economic growth in Morocco is forever hampered by a

high birth rate (over 3 percent) which continues to erase whatever short-term improvements that may be taking place in the agricultural and industrial sectors. On top of this the job market is expanding more slowly than the available manpower or skills. Unemployment ranges from 20 to 30 percent in the cities and averages 40 percent in the rural areas. Counting underemployment, the figure could be as high as 50 percent and will probably increase in the future.

The aspect of Morocco's economic development and planning that has the most serious implications for social and political stability is the ever-widening discrepancy between society's wealthy few and impovershed many. As reflected in current life styles and consumption patterns, the rich of Morocco are becoming more opulent while the poor are finding survival more difficult. In Casablanca, for example, the country's economic capital, luxurious villas with swimming pools and tennis courts are being built in a new elite suburb appropriately called California, while an estimated 25 percent of the city's population is unemployed and lives in shacks on the edge of the city or crowded in with relatives in the old part of the city. At present consumption levels it is estimated that 10 percent of the Moroccan population is absorbing 45 percent of the nation's wealth. Concurrently, economic expectations continue to rise among all sectors of the population resulting in increased frustrations. And despite the five year plan's call for a more equitable distribution of wealth, the government's agrarian reform program, for example, has been able to distribute only half of the projected million acres of farm land. Financial institutions, industry, and agriculture all form a close circle, bound together by corruption, spoils, inefficiency, and family ties, providing little outlet for a growing educated young generation and none for the unemployed and landless. In the absence of fundamental structural change, Morocco's economic future, like its political one, appears bleak.

FOREIGN POLICY

Foreign policy decision-making processes in Morocco are the monopoly of the system's narrowly stratified incumbent political elites revolving around the patrimonial authority of the monarch. While pluralistic tendencies are evident in certain sectors of Moroccan domestic life, no such pluralism exists concerning the articulation, deliberation, and implementation of foreign policy.

From this perspective Morocco's continued strong ties with France are in part a response to geopolitical and economic reality, in part a function of historical conditioning, but also a reflecton of the elites' intimate psychocultural affinity with French culture, language, and civilization. These latter characteristics are not shared by the population at large or even a great portion of its educated stratum, thereby highlighting the discontinuity between elite and mass political cultures and the incongruous policy outputs resulting from such cultural discontinuity. Thus it is uncertain to what extent the Moroccan people share in their government's strong pro-Western orientation especially its warm and friendly relations with the United States.

In reward for its "moderation" in world affairs, the United States has been the predominant supplier of military aid and a substantial contributor of economic assistance to post-independence Morocco. France remains Morocco's closest trading partner and provides the country with extensive technical, financial, and educational aid for which there is an urgent need. Relations with the Soviet Union are cordial and developing.

While it identifies with the larger aspirations of Arabs everywhere, including the call for Arab unity, opposition to Zionism, pride in a common cultural, religious, historical, and linguistic heritage, and a desire to assert an authentic Arab identity, Morocco is not directly involved in Middle Eastern affairs. In its own immediate area of the Maghrib, Morocco continues in an ideological and territorial dispute with Algeria. The most recent conflict involved the former territory of Spanish Sahara which was originally divided up between Morocco and Mauritania much to the chagrin of the Algerians who subsequently began to provide logistical and political support to the so-called Polisario Front, an amorphous tribal group of Sahara residents fighting against Morocco and, until recently, Mauritania in quest of an independent homeland in the desert.

Relations with Tunisia are amicable and becoming more so as both regimes begin to resemble each other more and more in terms of leadership style, ideology or, more accurately, nonideology, and developmental policies especially in the crucial areas of private foreign investment. The always unpredictable Colonel Qaddafi of Libya is highly distrusted by the monarchy, although probably admired by the average Moroccan, particularly since plots against the king including those that failed in 1971 and 1972, have been associated with Libyan-supported agents.

Because of the regime's dubious legitimacy among many disenchanted elements of the middle class, including students, professionals, intellectuals, workers, and unionist leaders, foreign policy issues are often invoked as a means of mobilizing support for the monarchy and distracting attention away from the many domestic ills besetting the country. Such was the case with the so-called "Green March" of 350,000 unarmed Moroccan civilians into the Spanish zone of the Sahara in late 1975, which did indeed manage to arouse new, albeit temporary, support for the king and his policies. Similarly, in April 1977, Hassan's decision to send elite paratroop units of Morocco's army to fight in Zaire in support of Mobutu's struggle against secessionist forces in Katanga province proved equally popular with the masses, especially since it involved virtually no loss of life and little expense. Again a foreign policy issue was used to the advantage of the regime in its continuing quest to assert its authority at home among an increasingly restive population.

Moroccan foreign policy, therefore, is less the result of objective geopolitical or economic considerations or a reflection of the popular will and political sentiments of the masses, but rather it is a means by which domestic political elites can maintain their dominant positions of power in the system. The success of such a policy has depended upon the cultivation of close economic, technical, and military ties with France and the United States while maintaining a symbolic association with the rest of the Afro-Arab world. As a consequence, Morocco's elite-generated foreign policy process is in danger of being fundamentally altered once the monarch or monarchy is overturned given the very low level of political institutionalization that has developed since independence.

In the meantime it can be expected that tensions with Algeria and, eventually, Spain, given the continued presence of the Spanish enclaves of Ceuta and Mellila on Moroccan soil, will continue. Verbal and symbolic affinity with the Arab world will be maintained unsupported by concrete action, and dependence on the United States and France for economic, technical, and military aid will increase, notwithstanding Morocco's official nonalignment position between the two superpowers and its efforts to establish a more balanced position in international affairs.

ALGERIA

POSTINDEPENDENCE POLITICS

THE SIGNING OF THE EVIAN ACCORDS with France in March 1962, spelled the successful conclusion of a bloody, revolutionary war that had lasted nearly eight years. Yet the surface unity that marked the FLN's (*Front de Libération Nationale*) military and diplomatic efforts broke down immediately at independence, a time which witnessed a vicious struggle for power among contending groups.

All the intrinsically fissiparous forces which had been accommodated within the FLN were unleashed once the principal goal of independence had been achieved. The three major contestants for power were the provisional government (*Gouvernement Provisoire de la République Algérienne* or GPRA), the *wilaya* commands (the Algerian commando units who fought within the country against the French and who were organized into six military operational zones or *wilayas*), and the army of the frontier or external army (the *Armée de Libération Nationale* or ALN, the established revolutionary army from 1954 to 1962 which was stationed in Morocco and Tunisia).

At issue were wartime misdemeanors, ideology, ethnic and clan ties, loyalties to specific individuals, and competing perspectives on the nature of post-independence Algerian society. At stake was the very center of political power in this society. The absence of mutual trust and confidence, a hallmark of Algerian political culture which was further nurtured during the nationalist and revolutionary periods, meant that competition would descend to the level of conflict where political survival would be involved. In short, the war had divided political power and authority among the *wilaya* leaders, the General Staff of the ALN, and the GPRA, while personal rivalries created additional divisions. The infighting among the FLN leaders themselves was bitter and not limited solely to political intrigues.

The first round in the postwar struggle was fought at the Tripoli (Libya) congress of the FLN National Council in May 1962, where the factionalism and deep-seated antagonism extant among all the principal nationalist leaders surfaced. The purpose of the Tripoli meeting was to elect a political bureau that would assume the control of the FLN and to draw up a political and economic program for independent Algeria. A commission headed by Ahmed Ben Bella, the head of the FLN, produced a document that was later to be called the Tripoli Program, which had three main objectives: the reform and modernization of agriculture, the decolonization of the economy, and industrialization for economic development within a planned socialist framework. In foreign policy the program aimed towards Maghrib unity, neutralism, and anticolonialism, especially in Africa. Despite the opposition of GPRA's President Ben Youcef Ben Khedda and his group, the Tripoli Program became the official policy of the FLN.

When the competing factions returned to Algeria, Ben Bella, with the military support of the ALN chief of staff, Colonel Houari Boumediene, was able to gain the initiative and establish his authority over party and nation. In the process complete civil war between loyal ALN forces and dissident *wilaya* leaders was averted partly because of mass demonstrations against the fighting organized by the Algerian General Worker's Union (*Union Générale des Travailleurs Algériens* or UGTA).

On September 20, 1962, elections for the National Assembly were held. All powers of the GPRA were transferred to the new assembly, and formal proclamation of the Democratic and Popular Republic of Algeria was made. Six days later the assembly elected Ben Bella premier and empowered him to form a government. He immediately formed a cabinet that included Boumediene as defense minister, others drawn from the ANP (*Armée Nationale Populaire,* the reconstituted name of the Algerian army after 1962) staff, and Ben Bella's personal and political associates.

The new government was thus established but still remained confronted by several oppositional forces including the remnant faction of Hajj Messali, the discredited Communist Party, and the left-wing socialists of Mohamed Boudiaf, all of whom were officially banned by November 1962. The old military *wilaya* system was eliminated, although the term *wilaya* was later used for the local administrative districts. Other potential opposition surfaced among the students and UGTA, but by January 1963, these groups, too, were under the firm control of the FLN.

Once the new government had consolidated its position, it set about attacking the severe economic plight of the country caused in great part by the sudden and massive exodus of the Europeans, representing virtually all the entrepreneurs, technicians, administrators, teachers, doctors, and skilled workers. With factories, farms, and shops closed, more than 70 percent of the population was left unemployed. In March 1963, overwhelmed by the catastrophic economic situation and unguided by any particular socialist ideology, Ben Bella signed into law several decrees ("the March Decrees") which legalized the takeover of extensive agricultural and industrial properties abandoned (*biens vacants*) in the exodus and instituted the system of *autogestion,* or workers' management.

Autogestion was conceived as an economic system based on workers' management of their own affairs through elected officials and cooperation with the state through a director and national agencies. The state had the function of guiding, counseling, and coordinating their activities within the framework of an evolving national plan. *Autogestion* was seen as a stage in the transformation from a colonial to a socialist economy. The guiding forces during the transition were designated as the peasants, workers, and revolutionary intellectuals united in the tasks of planned social action, civic formation, and economic development. This, then, was to become the pillar of Algerian socialism or *option socialiste:* the *vacant* agricultural means of production had been converted from the private property of the settlers to the collective property of the workers and society as a whole. Unfortunately, the severe shortage of qualified personnel and the inability of workers and peasants to fully comprehend the principles of self-management made this bold experiment in socialism more a myth than a reality. Nonetheless, given the relative backwardness of the working class and peasantry, the fact that *autogestion* was installed and worked at all in the early years was a significant development.

Yet Ben Bella's style of governance was unable to instill confidence among a war-weary population. Politically educated in an atmosphere of clandestine national plotting and reflecting the broader cultural traits of suspicion, distrust, and conspiratorial thinking, Ben Bella proved to be a divisive rather than unifying leader. In April 1963, for example, he increased his power and personal standing when he took over the post of general secretary of the FLN. In August Ben Bella secured the adoption by the assembly of a draft constitution providing for a presidential regime, with the FLN as the sole political party. The new constitution was approved in a referendum on September 8, and became effective September 10, 1963. Three days later Ben Bella was elected president for a period of five years, assuming the title of commander-in-chief as well as becoming head of state and head of government.

This further consolidation of personal power and apparent move towards dictatorial government aroused opposition and the reemergence of factionalism. For example, the president of the assembly, Ferhat Abbas, the leading spokesman for a more liberal policy, resigned from the presidency and was subsequently expelled from the FLN. In the Kabyle, where discontent was accentuated by Berber regionalism, sporadic disturbances broke out and a revolt had to be quashed by police action and political compromise. Partly in an attempt to regain popularity, in October 1963, Ben Bella placed more French estates under *autogestion* and suppressed the remaining French-controlled newspapers.

In April 1964, the long-awaited first congress of the FLN was held in Algiers, despite opposition from right-wing forces and the negative indifference of the army. The purpose of the congress was to sort out the ideological differences among various competing groups within the ruling establishment. Towards this end the Algiers Charter, as the FLN ideological platform came to be called, was formally adopted. It was the most complete analysis of the social and economic situation in Algeria yet to be undertaken and the most far-ranging program the FLN had ever produced. Echoing the Tripoli Program, the charter analyzed past mistakes of the party, including the conflicts that had divided the leadership of the FLN and influenced the party's policies during the war. It also defined relations between the state, party, and army, and gave support to the presentation of traditional Islamic principles as theoretical guidelines for Algerian socialism and its *autogestion* component.

Although it did not fulfill Ben Bella's hope of establishing a basis for a homogeneous socialist party, the congress did have several important political consequences for the Algerian leader. First, it completed the process of legitimizing his seizure of power, strengthening his hand against the opposition; second, it completed the split between him and the army;

and, finally, it prepared the way for an alliance with leftist groups outside the FLN which had strongly endorsed the Algiers Charter. Most important, however, was that the congress set into motion the feud between Ben Bella and Boumediene which was eventually to culminate in the *coup de main* of June 19, 1965. Ben Bella attempted to strengthen the leftist organizations in the hope that this would strengthen him against the army, while Boumediene tried to resolve the conflict between the *wilaya* leaders and the new officers of the ANP in the hope of unifying the army against Ben Bella.

Despite his numerous efforts at institutionalization of the revolution and its socialist ideology, Ben Bella was never able to overcome the many rivalries, challenges, and contests that faced his regime. In addition, his ouster of the traditional leaders, his hostility to the UGTA in the form of repeated political attacks, his failure to make the FLN an efficient mass party, his suspicion of plotters behind every door, and his increasingly dictatorial tendencies alienated many political leaders and interest groups. Once the army turned against him he was left virtually powerless and completely vulnerable. On the eve of the Afro-Asian conference that was scheduled to take place in Algeria, Colonel Boumediene and his supporters deposed and arrested Ben Bella in a swift and bloodless *coup de main*. The June 19, 1965, military takeover hardly caused a ripple in Algerian society as power was smoothly and efficiently transferred to Boumediene and a Council of the Revolution which was designated as the supreme political body. Despite his popularity among the masses and his status as one of the "historic chiefs" of the revolution, Ben Bella's constant improvisation rather than careful planning offended even his close supporters who eventually turned against him in the June coup led by the very man who had been instrumental in originally establishing Ben Bella's power base during the internecine conflicts of the immediate post-independence period.

Under the authority of the Council of the Revolution, a new government of twenty members, consisting mostly of military figures, was announced on July 10, 1965, with Boumediene as prime minister and minister of defense and Abdelaziz Bouteflika continuing as foreign minister. According to the council, the aims of the new regime was to reestablish the principles of the revolution, to remedy the abuses of personal power associated with Ben Bella, to end internal divisions, and to create an "authentic" socialist society based on a sound economy. Boumediene's base of support differed significantly from that of his predecessor who had depended on the workers, the peasants, and the leftist intellectuals. Boumediene relied on the veterans of the war of independence (*mujahidin*), the ALN officers, and a new class of young technocrats to constitute the system's dynamic political force. This choice of appropriate "revolutionary forces" reflected Boumediene's more somber and low-key style of authority. At heart the shy, introverted Boumediene was a reformist and organizer who stressed the need for planning and reflection and was wary of radical change. This was evident in the 1965–67 years which could be called the period of transition when the regime's internal political and social direction seemed somewhat hesitant and its legitimacy not yet tested. There was little attempt, for example, to resuscitate national political life and the Algerian National Assembly remained in abeyance while the FLN remained moribund. Municipal elections were held in February 1967, in keeping with Boumediene's strategy of constructing a political system from the base and developing popular institutions locally and regionally as a prelude to the establishment of national institutions. The elections to the *Assemblées Populaires Communales* (APC), the local level legislative assemblies, could hardly be interpreted as an expression of confidence in the revolutionary council, however, given the low voter turnouts and many blank ballots cast. Yet with these elections the council had taken its first concrete step towards reestablishing legal institutions in the country, and it had begun a badly needed reform of the administration.

Neither these elections nor the six-day Arab-Israeli War of June 1967, managed to hold off the latent conflicts still present among the various groups competing for power, including certain left-wing ministers, the UGTA, the students, and some sections of the army, notably the former *wilaya* leaders. These feared the imposition of a technocratic and centralized form of socialism, different from the syndicalist concepts embodied in *autogestion,* and felt that collegial rule was being supplanted by the dictatorship of the small group around Boumediene.

This opposition took violent form when, on December 14, 1967, Colonel Tahar Zbiri, army chief of staff and a prominent former *wilaya* leader, launched an armed uprising in the countryside. This was quickly and efficiently put down by forces loyal to Boumediene. Other groups, especially dissident students, continued to show their opposition to the new regime by going on strike and holding street demonstrations. In the Aurès and Kabyle regions as well, there were reports of guerrilla activity. And on April 25, 1968, there was an unsuccessful attempt to assassinate Boumediene, who escaped with only minor injuries. This latter incident may have constituted a symbolic turning point for the regime's legitimacy and stability.

In fact, from 1968 to 1972 the regime managed to successfully consolidate its power, enabling it to initiate bold policies of development in the industrial, agricultural, and political fields. The second stage of the reform of governmental institutions, for example, was put into operation in May 1969, when the *wilaya* or regional level assembly (*Assemblées Populaires de Wilaya* or APW) elections took place, reflecting the regime's increasing sense of political confidence. Both the February 1967 APC elections and May 1969 APW elections gave clear indication of how Boumediene envisioned the organization of the Algerian state and its political institutions. Specifically, his idea was to have a system of decentralized local government counterbalanced by a single centralized party (FLN) and a well-established administration.

It was also during this period that the regime gave priority to the development of heavy industry, particularly of the oil and gas industry. The official rationale for this policy was that Algeria must become totally independent of foreign aid and investment capital as quickly as possible. The country's first four-year development plan (1970–1973) was launched in this period as well. It emphasized the establishment of a capital-intensive sector, involving the hydrocarbon, iron and steel, chemical, and engineering industries, which was to serve as a basis for economic growth. The plan allocated 45 percent of investments to industry, 15 percent to agriculture, and 40 percent to social and economic infrastructure. At the end of 1971 a major effort was also made to improve the increasingly serious situation in traditional agriculture which hitherto had been purposely reduced to a secondary position behind industrial development. Major agrarian reform legislation was promulgated to reorganize the distribution of land in that sector.

In both the transitional (1965–1967) and consolidation (1968–1971) periods, the Boumediene regime pursued a calculated policy of "depoliticization"; that is, the authorities worked to explicitly remove the masses from active political participation so as to devote full energies to economic development, especially industrialization. In the most recent phase (1972–1977) a more balanced approach towards the simultaneous development of the industrial, agricultural, and political-governmental fields has been adopted via a process of careful socialization and evolutionary institutionalization. While the second four-year plan (1974–1977), for example, still pays attention to the heavy industry base, more emphasis is being placed on housing and health and on training, as well as on labor-intensive projects, small and medium-sized industries, and on improved agricultural methods, with the aim of achieving a greater degree of self-sufficiency in foodstuffs.

It is in the political sphere, however, that incipient changes appear to be taking place. The virtual absence of meaningful political representation and popular participation in the first half decade of Boumediene's rule, save the installation and operation of the APC's and APW's which, however, were given little authority and responsibility, led the Algerian leader to critically reassess the status of the nation's political institutions, particularly its single party governing structure, the FLN. While the regime had successfully created a stable political environment within which the dynamics of sociopolitical change could take place, this had been achieved at the expense of politics itself. The FLN, for all intent and purposes, had been allowed to become a moribund and overly bureaucratized political apparatus designed more, in fact, to monopolize formal political life on behalf of its ruling elite and prevent potentially dissident political activity than to serve its stated purpose of giving policy direction to the government's operation. Now, however, there have been signs that the party organ and national political life at large are being revitalized, reflecting in part the growing political confidence achieved by the regime and its leader in a decade and a half of uncontested rule. On the tenth anniversary of his assumption of power (June 19, 1975), for example, Boumediene announced the preparation of a national charter and constitution which would provide the theoretical basis of the political institutions that were to be created and/or reactivated.

This was followed, nearly a year later in May 1976, by animated public debate and government-directed political renewal. The draft of the charter was made the subject of extensive and surprisingly candid discussion in party gatherings, trade union meetings, and assemblies of the burgeoning peasants' association, all reflecting widening public participation in political life while reaffirming the power of Boumediene and his regime. On June 27, 1976, the National Charter was approved by a referendum in which, according to official figures, 98.51 percent of the electorate voted "yes," in a poll of 91.36. This latest Algerian national charter—the three previous included the Charter of Soummam, adopted in August 1956, the Tripoli Program (June 1962), and the Algiers Charter, voted upon by the FLN Congress in April 1964—is conceived as a grand ideological inventory of Algeria's socialist history and the future directions the country will pursue. It also delineates in detail the popular and institutional basis of the future Algeria giving renewed prominence to the FLN as the nation's only "authentic" representative of the people's will and as the country's avant-garde political institution. In addition, the participatory role of citizens in a socialist society is stressed. The remarkable degree of open political debate and public criticism of inefficient bureaucracy, corruption, and economic inequality that was articulated in the government-controlled press, party meetings, and huge rallies preceding both the National Charter and, later, constitution referendums provide a certain amount of practical credibility to the charter's encouragement and protection of citizens' political rights and obligations.

Less than six months after approving the National Charter, the electorate, on November 20, 1976, once again went to the polls and overwhelmingly approved a new constitution restoring a national assembly (*Assemblée Populaire Nationale* or APN) and an elected president. This marked the official return to constitutional life which had been suspended since a July 10, 1965, ordinance abrogated the 1963 constitution promulgated under Ben Bella. A lengthy document with a preamble and 199 articles, this newest constitution provides the government with new institutional machinery. In general terms the return of constitutional government lessened Boumediene's dependence on a small circle of military men and allowed him to govern as an elected head of state with institutionalized authority over the government, the army, and the FLN. Since Boumediene personally led and encouraged the public debate in favor of the two new documents, the votes approving them were, in fact, votes of confidence in the man himself and his system of rule.

Ostensibly the new constitution returns the country to civilian control. Yet unlike the assembly that existed before the coup of June 1965, the APN is not empowered to vote censure of the president and force his resignation. According to Article 108 the president serves a six-year term with no limit on reelection.

Less than a month after approval of the constitution, Boumediene was elected president of the republic with more than 99.5 percent of the vote in a turnout of 96 percent. While he ran unopposed and was, in fact, the only candidate on the ballot, the December 10, 1976, presidential election, the first in thirteen years, was authentically reflective of the people's will. Under the constitution Boumediene became officially head of state, head of government, commander-in-chief of the armed forces, head of national defense, and nominally the head of the FLN, all of which significantly enhance an institutional power that was already well fortified by unquestioning military support.

Finally, as provided for in the new constitution, legislative elections for the new National Assembly took place on February 25, 1977. Surprisingly, only 78.5 percent of the registered voters turned out for Algeria's first parliamentary election since 1962 to choose among 783 candidates vying for 261 parliamentary seats, not on issues but rather on criteria of "competence, integrity, and commitment" to Algeria's socialist revolution.

Although all of the candidates were chosen by the FLN, there was a certain amount of debate between the grass-roots militants and the party leadership over the choices. The elected representatives to a five-year term of the new APN included six government ministers, diplomats, army officers, peasants, industry and office workers, civil servants, party workers, and several women. Stressing that the new APN was composed of a majority of peasants and workers, government officials described the APN as the final step in the construction of a socialist state which began a decade earlier with communal (APC) elections. Undoubtedly, the complexity of electoral procedures and the rapid succession of national referendums help explain in part the relatively low voter turnout. Nonetheless, the system-wide process of participatory politics has now been set into motion and institutionalized in two detailed and formally approved documents which makes it highly unlikely that unrepresentative, authoritarian rule can reemerge without causing major unrest among a newly politicized mass public.

This did not mean, however, that Boumediene voluntarily relinquished his extensive powers. A new government formed on April 27, 1977, for example, was composed of twenty-four ministers and three secretaries of state, all of whom were considered the "president's men," loyal, obedient, and, for the most part, competent. The first government of this new constitutional system, now designated as the Second Algerian Republic (the First Republic was from 1963 to 1965), concentrated constitutionally defined power in the president. Since he did not designate a prime minister, a constitutional prerogative of his office, and already held the titles of head of state, government, party, defense, and army, Boumediene has confirmed his authority and significantly enhanced the prospects for an enduring legitimacy for a socialist system that confronts many serious economic, social, and developmental problems.

Beyond creating the important institutional and participatory bases of Algerian political life, Boumediene's main accomplishments as leader of Algeria during the past years have included: stabilizing the nation's leadership, consolidating government control over the economy, introducing comprehensive economic planning, capitalizing on oil and gas revenues, and generally aiming at rapid industrialization.

With the sudden and unexpected death of Boumediene on December 27, 1978, of a rare blood disease, executive power was constitutionally transferred to Rabah Bitat, president of the National Assembly and the only remaining politically active member of the revolution's original nine "historic chiefs." Article 117 of the 1976 constitution stipulates that in case of the death or resignation of the president the incumbent head of the APN is automatically designated interim chief of state for forty-five days until new presidential elections take place. Such elections are to be held under the organizational and political auspices of the FLN in an extraordinary session convened especially for purposes of selecting a presidential candidate. The head of the National Assembly is constitutionally prohibited from running as a candidate for the presidency.

In its fourth party congress held on January 27–31, 1979, the FLN convened 3,290 delegates representing various political, professional, military, labor, and governmental groups. Presidential aspirations were contested in the numerous committee meetings and closed sessions of the five-day party congress with several political factions emerging and revolving around the following individuals within the Council of the Revolution: Mohamed Salah Yahyiaoui, former commander of the prestigious Cherchell Military Academy and, since October 1977, administrative head of the FLN, who represented left-wing interests with an emphasis on accelerated Arabization, hard-line socialism, Islamic fundamentalism, and continued Soviet friendship. Foreign Minister Bouteflika's relatively moderate posture, pro-Western sympathies, and call for greater liberalization of Algerian society had the support of a handful of key council members including the powerful minister of the interior, Mohamed Ben Ahmed Abdelghani. Colonel Ahmed Bencherif, the hydraulics minister and former *gendarmerie* commandant, represented himself but with the outside support of several influential military figures in the Ministry of Defense. Finally, Colonel Chadli Benjedid, informally representing army-national interests which are normally viewed as standing above any parochial or special political considerations, constituted the "independent" candidate who had the full backing of the 640-member military (ANP) delegation to the congress.

On the last day of the congress the so-called "moderate majority" defeated a movement by leftists to gain greater influence in the FLN's leadership by selecting the powerful and respected head of the Oran military region, Chadli Benjedid, as the new secretary-general of the party and the only candidate for the February 7, 1979, presidential election. With the confirmation of election results on February 9 (94.23 percent approval of the electorate), Chadli assumed the presidency as the country's third elected head of state.

Unlike Boumediene's concentrated personal powers and wide-ranging authority—at the time of his incapacitation in fall 1978 he still held the following positions: president of the republic, president of the Council of the Revolution, president of the Council of Ministers, head of the army, minister of defense (since 1963), and head of the FLN—the new president's powers have been significantly reduced. This is the result of the creation of a 17-member Political Bureau of the FLN, 160-member Central Committee (30 alternates), a prime minister selected by the central committee rather than the president, as had been the case under Boumediene who never invoked this prerogative, and the option of selecting up to three vice-presidents.

Since his election to the presidency Chadli has pursued a cautious, middle-of-the road policy consistent with his strong military identification and institutional loyalty that made him, during the critical January party congress, a perfect symbol of the army as guarantor and arbiter of the national interest. His personal image reinforced this—Arabo-Muslim in cultural orientation, a nationalist unsullied by intrigue. Chadli's nomination reflected the army's determination to protect its own place at the very center of Algerian politics by preventing a marked shift of power to either the state (Bouteflika) or the party (Yahyiaoui).

The creation of an enlarged political bureau and the election of a central committee of the FLN along with the formation of a new government of twenty-nine ministers in March 1979, have provided further insight into the policy and personnel configuration of the new regime. For example, the initial hesitancy to tamper with Boumediene's political legacy coupled with Chadli's uncertain national status have quickly given way to more pronounced political designs that reflect both the continuity and change that have been the hallmarks of post-independence Algeria. Within the narrow ruling elite circle the anticipated "power struggle," predicted by many in the immediate post-succession period, seems to have gotten under way if, indeed, it has not already been terminated all in rather swift fashion. The post-Boumediene continuity apparent, for example, in the make-up of the FLN's seventeen-member Politburo has been "balanced" by changes evident with the appointment of the new government in which Yahyiaoui's power and influence seem to have expanded, indirectly at least, along with those of Prime Minister Mohamed Ben Ahmed Abdelghani both at the expense of the moderate, pro-Western Bouteflika and his supporters.

One immediate consequence of this seeming realignment is that power is now effectively redistributed among Chadli (army), Yahyiaoui (party), and Abdelghani (government), eliminating in the process the single-man concentration of authority which for so long characterized Boumediene's system of rule. In theory at least, the premiership and the party leadership now constitute alternative bases of power. Yet all three men have common military origins and associations— indeed, that Chadli, Abdelghani, and Yahyiaoui all hold the rank of colonel, the highest rank in the Algerian army, is reminder that the ANP has not surrendered its influence— and share in the belief of the supremacy of a strong and secure state.

Postindependence Algeria has evolved into a bureaucratic polity; a political system in which power and national decision-making are shaped almost exclusively by the employees of the state, and especially by the topmost levels of the officer corps, single party organization, and civilian bureaucracy, including the significant socioeconomic class of managers and technicians. It is this complex political legacy that Boumediene has bequeathed to his successor, Chadli Benjedid.

POLITICAL CULTURE AND IDEOLOGY

As elsewhere in the Maghrib elite political culture differs markedly from mass political culture in Algeria. To the extent that the masses are cognizant of belief systems at all, they identify unswervingly with Islam and its religious symbols. It is only in the relatively small "modernized" sector and its even smaller elite component that one finds political culture and ideology as at all meaningfull categories of analysis. As would be expected, therefore, those Algerians who must deal with power and have responsibilities for the decisions of government invariably develop outlooks on politics different from those in the society who remain simply observers or marginal activists.

Algerian political culture reflects the impact of both general cultural values and of recent historical experiences, especially the revolutionary war, on the men who have assumed leadership positions in the state. From both these environments has emerged a conflictual political culture where intraelite hostility and mistrust predominate. Somewhat like their Moroccan counterparts, Algerian politicians often behave, and expect others to behave, as if they are constantly maneuvering and scheming to acquire more power. The pejorative term *boulitique*—an Arabic dialectical borrowing and transformation of the French word *politique*—has come to describe this characteristic brand of elite political behavior in Algeria.

One immediate consequence of *boulitique* is the personalization of political differences where personal rivalries and personal clashes substitute for legitimate political discourse. Another consequence of this attitude is the distrust of any form of political opposition which, in combination with the debilitating intraelite conflicts that took place during and immediately after the war for independence, has led Algerian politicians to see any form of public political disagreement as harmful and illegitimate to the political process. Hence the persistent effort to create homogeneous ruling groups that can insure political stability. Yet even this attitude may be changing as over ten years of "homogeneous" rule has led Boumediene and his successor regime to encourage and even articulate the need for "legitimate" dissent and a free expression of opposing opinions. The animated debates over the National Charter, for example, were remarkably open, candid, and, in some cases, brutal. While this experience does not foreshadow the rise of liberal democracy, it may represent a modification in the previously conspiratorial and unitary mentality so characteristic of incumbent elites. It also may feed off another, paradoxical aspect of Algerian political culture, namely the strong feeling that—widespread distrust of one's colleagues in politics notwithstanding—political relations must be based on equality and reciprocity. Despite the apparent contradictions and tensions inherent in such an inconsistent perspective, it continues to coexist in the minds of many Algerian leaders.

The most noteworthy expression of this demand for equality is found in the notion of collegial rule and for consultation, and in the rejection of the idea of a "cult of personality." This latter trait was the most damning accusation made against Ben Bella. Boumediene and now Chadli, on the other hand, have emphasized collegiality and consultation, albeit among a narrow group of political advisers, technocrats, and military men.

This mixture of distrust and egalitarianism in political life is often explained away by the so-called individualistic nature of Algerians. That is, the fact that Algerians both distrust those who have power and demand an equal share of influence for themselves is attributed to their individualism. Yet this individualism, manifest at times in a kind of public rebellion and sporadic violence, belies an underlying pressure to conform: to rigorous norms that must be followed, social codes that must be obeyed, and a public opinion that must be paid due reverence. The compelling need to conform and the private docility that it engenders undermine the meaning of individualism, as it is understood in the West at least—innovative behavior, tolerance for deviance, willingness to break with tradition—in Algerian political life.

As intraelite relations are marked by coexisting contradictory impulses, so too are the attitudes toward the proper role of government characterized by fundamentally inconsistent views.

The colonial and war experiences have had particularly profound impact on the elites' perception of the "proper" role of government. Specifically, there is a general belief in the need for a strong centralized state often referred to as

.

state capitalism or *étatisme* when applied to economic development and organization. Simultaneously, and in apparent contradiction, Algerian political culture places great stress on the role of the impoverished masses reflecting a populist orientation. The principles and practices of *autogestion* in agriculture and industry, although significantly reduced since 1967, exemplify the meaning of populism in the economic sphere.

In its essentials populism consists of two fundamental principles: first, the supremacy of the will of the people which is identified with justice and morality above all other norms; and secondly, the importance of a direct relationship between the people and their leaders in which intermediary institutions and mediating structures can play no meaningful role.

These unreconciled perceptions of the role of government originate from a strongly felt sense of nationalism and a less clearly defined attachment to the rhetoric and symbolism, and much less frequently also to the content, of socialism. Among the political elite these dual notions of nationalism and socialism have assumed sacrosanct status. The *étatiste* policies of Algerian developmental elites are, in fact, justified in nationalist terms wherein the state is viewed as having the "right" to intervene in many areas of national life. In particular, it is felt that the state must control its own resources and territory. Yet there remains a genuine commitment to the masses which transcends the excessive revolutionary and socialist rhetoric. This is reflected in the areas of welfare, education, and social services where government policy has been "progressive" and enlightened. There is also a commitment to the idea of eventual mass political participation and administrative decentralization as the National Charter debates, new constitution, and presidential and legislative elections in 1976–77 have demonstrated.

Other elements of political culture and ideology in Algeria

include belief in a continuing revolution, Arab unity, and the resurrection of an Algerian Arab-Islamic culture through the means of Arabization and under the guidance of a mass mobilization political party. The Islamic component of socialism remains a salient feature of contemporary ideology. For Algerian ideologues socialism can have no meaning outside the realm of Islamic belief. In the Algerian context socialism refers to a belief system whereby a centralized structure is concerned with the allocation of resources and whose objective is the control and utilization of national economic wealth so as to prevent one class from monopolizing the products. Yet this takes place within the world of Islam which constitutes the "heart, mind, and soul" of Algerian consciousness. Thus not only is there no apparent contradiction between scientific socialism and religious belief, but in fact the former has no meaning outside the Islamic essence of Algerian national and cultural identity. This perspective is reaffirmed in both the National Charter and new constitution which explicitly extol Islamic socialism as the road to political, economic, social, and cultural salvation. Earlier political documents including the Tripoli Program, the 1963 constitution, and the Algiers Charter were attempts at institutionalizing this Islamic socialist concept.

In practical terms this has permitted incumbent leaders to sustain a conservative, indeed puritanical policy in the area of personal, religious, and moral affairs while simultaneously pursuing a radical modernization policy involving rapid and sweeping economic growth, the use of advanced technology and scientific know-how, and dependence on western secularists for administrative, organizational, and financial expertise. Inevitably, the coexistence of socialist revolutionary, French republican, and Arab-Berber-Islamic-traditional influences generate unexpected tensions and contradictions which the current rulers have not yet satisfactorily reconciled, notwithstanding the long step forward taken in the National Charter and constitution.

By way of summary and conclusion, Algerian political culture can be described as containing several contradictory elements. There is, for example, the high level of mistrust and the expectation that reciprocity and equality will be respected characterizing intraelite relations. In addition, in terms of the elites' perception of the proper role of government, a strong statist orientation, growing out of intense nationalism, coexists with a populist orientation which emphasizes extensive mass participation and governmental decentralization. Finally, there is support for total Arabization and for the practice and perhaps imposition of ascetic, rigid, and austere Islamic orthodoxy coexisting within a nationalist milieu. This seeks to implement rapid and sweeping economic and social modernization, that is, Westernization at the expense of Arabization.

In terms of ideology, both empirical and affective socialism coexist under the rubric of Islamic socialism. Despite the ongoing excessive rhetoric surrounding socialist principles, it appears that a broad consensus has emerged concerning an overall socialist orientation. This orientation has been provisionally institutionalized with the reactivation of parliamentary, constitutional, and party life. Socialist ideology thus enables the government not only to reject the West and to identify with other "radical" Arab states but also to reject certain aspects of local tradition found to be obstacles to social progress. Through numerous government-controlled propaganda organs and the communications media the regime has continued to advance a socialist program aimed primarily at building up the economic strength of the state, particularly raising the standards of living of its rural and urban populations, and at providing a framework for rapid industrialization and agrarian reform.

POLITICAL STRUCTURES

The 1965 coup suspended the National Assembly and constitution established under Ben Bella in 1962 and 1963, respectively. At the national level for over a decade thereafter, Algerian political life was strongly centralized under the Council of the Revolution and the Council of Ministers, both headed by Boumediene. In the absence of a constitution, the Council of Ministers became responsible for the day-to-day administration of the government and thus became the effective executive and legislative body. The FLN and other national-level institutions were allowed to atrophy in order that Boumediene's vision of a strong, secure, centralized government could evolve free of the challenge that such organizations could present. Instead, he believed that institutional development could only emerge from the base up via a systematic process of political education.

In accordance with this strategy, communal (APC) elections first took place in February 1967, and were renewed in February 1971 and December 1979. Likewise, regional (APW) elections were held in May 1969, five years later in May 1974, and most recently in December 1979, when 71.35 percent of the APW registered voters participated in the elections. However, these local and regional level assemblies are largely administrative in function without significant political authority. A congress of the presidents of these assemblies is held annually and, although there is no juridical basis for these meetings, they have attained quasi-institutional status.

In formal administrative terms Algeria is divided into 31 *wilayas* (regional administrative entities) which are further subdivided into *da'iraat* or districts, and 704 communes or *baladiyat,* the smallest administrative units. Each *wilaya* is administered by a *wali* (governor) who is appointed by decree and is responsible to the minister of the interior.

Despite the regime's claim that the assemblies were created with the objective of instituting a greater measure of self-government at the local level, more accurately these local and regional groupings have served to reorganize and strengthen the national system of political control and population integration. Their claim to political autonomy, for example, as demonstrated in the several elections that have taken place is undermined by the numerous obstacles to the growth of political life that are still present. For example, while the elections permit choice between candidates—there being, as prescribed by the system, twice as many candidates as seats to be filled—all of the candidates are nominated by the FLN. There is no competition between parties, nor do candidates engage in an electoral contest, since campaigning is the work of FLN notables and ministers. All this results in politically lethargic and administratively marginal local-level associations that depend on the central authorities for guidance and animation.

Either because the system of assemblies had succeeded well enough or failed altogether, Boumediene began in the early 1970s to call for greater politicization of the masses by advocating renewed involvement in the FLN as the sole ideological and institutional organ of the socialist revolution and later, in mid-1976, by personally directing the revival of constitutional politics in the form of public debates prior to the voting on the National Charter. The nationwide referendums voting in the National Charter and constitution in June and November 1976, respectively, represented the formal reestablishment of national institutional life.

The new constitution consists of a preamble and 199 articles of which 38 deal with legislative functions, 35 with individual liberties, 8 with duties and obligations of citizens, and 22 with powers of the executive. Articles 10 through 24 of the document's second chapter are dedicated to achieving Islamic socialism in Algeria. The constitution also states that no constitutional amendment can alter the republican nature of the state, the state religion which is Islam, the socialist system, or the territorial integrity of the country. The document also reaffirms state control of the means of production, land reforms, free medical care, worker participation in industry, and campaigns against corruption and nepotism. It guarantees that so-called "non-exploitative" private property of artisans, small farmers, and traders who live on their own work, will be respected. The constitution also guarantees the "liberation of women and their full participation in the political, economic, social and cultural life of the nation" and freedom of expression and assembly.

Executive powers are extensive and are vested in the president of the republic, who is elected for a six-year term by direct, adult suffrage and can be reelected for an unlimited number of terms. While the day-to-day administration of government is the responsibility of the cabinet (Council of Ministers), the president has the power to enact laws by decree when the legislature is not in session. A new institution to be set up under the constitution is the High Council of Security, charged with giving advice to the president on all questions affecting national security.

On December 10, 1976, Boumediene was overwhelmingly elected as the Second Algerian Republic's first president under the new constitution. A second presidential election on Februray 7, 1979, voted in Chadli Benjedid.

Legislative authority is spelled out in articles 126–163 of the constitution. The unicameral legislature is entitled the National Popular Assembly (*Assemblée Populaire Nationale* or APN) and its members are elected by secret, direct, and universal suffrage under the banner of the FLN for a period of five years. On Februray 24, 1977, the first legislative elections in well over a decade took place with 783 FLN-sponsored candidates vying for the 261 available parliamentary seats. It is yet too early to determine whether the new APN will be permitted to act as a forum for serious political debate or whether it will simply serve as the regime's bureaucratic rubber stamp unwilling or unable to act independently or decisively.

The judicial system in Algeria is in the process of transition from the French legal system. All civil, criminal, public, and family laws remaining from the preindependence era are being reviewed by a National Commission on Legislation. The Supreme Court has been retained under the revised system as the highest judicial authority. A state security court has been created to try individuals for crimes against the state. In addition, a series of tribunals for economic crimes against the state have also been established. Finally, the code dealing with family and personal status continues to be based on Muslim law but administered by the civil courts.

Fifteen years after independence, Algeria has established a series of national, regional, and local political and administrative structures that enhance the system's legitimacy and effectiveness. The setting up of a new constitution based on a comprehensive ideological blueprint called the National Charter along with the revival of the FLN as the sole organ of political association and participation further institutionalizes Algeria's socialist system. Finally, the successful completion of presidential and legislative elections paves the way for a more predictable and accountable form of government that transcends any particular individual or group. Obviously, it is still too early to determine whether or not these democratically defined political structures will be permanently institutionalized and legitimated among the Algerian people or simply will be ignored, misused, or undermined by authoritarian leadership. One thing seems certain, however, is that as long as these political structures remain in effect and despite some of the elite political culture's debilitating characteristics, it seems unlikely that an authoritarian regime, unresponsive to the people, can long remain. At minimum, the new political structures now in place should encourage the development of a relatively more open political process which will permit considerable mass participation.

POLITICAL PROCESSES

Algerian political processes in the post-independence period have been dominated by a small civil-military oligarchy with remarkably little participation on the part of the masses. This latter situation may be changing, however, as a consequence of the regime's policy of deliberate institutionalization and mobilization undertaken with full force in 1976–1977. Notwithstanding the future performance of such popular institutions as the national, regional, and local assemblies (APN, APW, and APC, respectively) and the revitalized mass party (FLN), power remains concentrated in the hands of a technocratic elite whose claim to authority is based on the modern skills that they possess and for which there is a high value in the society.

This technocratic system is made up of three major units which, while they have very different internal characteristics, are united in an overriding new allegiance to the state and its developmental objectives. The military, party, and administrative technocrats, who all share a common socializing background in the National Liberation Army (ALN) and its experience in the revolutionary war, monopolize the state's critical military, mobilization, and managerial affairs. Boumediene depended on this triumvirate to maintain and aggrandize power as well as to erect his socialist state using the crucial technical skills that this group possesses. For nearly a decade, however, these elements were unevenly aligned, with the FLN reduced to a minor, functionary role while the military and the administrative elite elevated to predominate positions. If the language of the National Charter and 1976 constitution is to be believed and the new parliament to be taken seriously, then an apparent balancing of forces may be taking place to the relative advantage of the hitherto much maligned and often ignored single party.

The *military* remains the most decisive force in Algerian politics today, particularly since the old dissensions between the *mujahidin* or *wilayists,* who fought in the interior of the country during the war of independence, and the established revolutionary army or ALN were resolved in favor of the latter. The ALN was renamed the Algerian People's Army in 1963. The army's claim to privileged status is not limited to the fact that it monopolizes the nation's coercive instruments of force or that Boumediene was the former chief of staff of the wartime ALN. (As defense minister and head of the army, Boumediene provided the critical support that brought Ben Bella to power only to be overthrown by Boumediene himself in a military *coup d'état.*) Equally important has been the fact that the military continues to possess a revolutionary mystique; that it was determinative in imposing law and order in the chaos that followed independence; that it possesses the special skills of organization and management that has enabled society to stabilize and develop; that it has become directly involved in local, rural affairs thus gaining popular support at the mass level; and that it firmly believes that it alone is the guardian of the revolution.

Despite the numerous advantages it possesses vis-à-vis other elite groups in the society, the military has so far played a guardian role getting involved directly in politics only when the situation required. It did so in 1962 when the external ALN coalesced behind Ben Bella in his struggle for power with the GPRA and dissident *wilaya* leaders; and it intervened again in 1965 following Ben Bella's attempt after the 1964 FLN party congress to remove military representation from the Council of Ministers which led the military to remove him instead. Aside from these two examples of direct army intervention, the military has followed a policy of "returning to the barracks" to observe the political process carefully and with a discrete hand.

Besides its explicitly military fuctions, the army is called upon to buttress the educational and literacy corps that are sent to the countryside to improve the educational level of the peasants. Like the U.S. Army Corps of Engineers, so too is the Algerian army called upon to assist in building dams, constructing roads, putting up telephone poles, and erecting health and medical facilities. The military is thus directly involved in the state-building process and as such further enhances its already wide popular appeal among the rural masses. Its representation in all elite political institutions, including the Council of Ministers, the National Assembly, and FLN permits the military to oversee directly all political activities. Finally, the qualitative and quantitative improvement in manpower and equipment which has been evident since the 1967 Arab-Israeli War, when Soviet military assistance and training increased noticeably, has made the Algerian military a credible threat and a force to contend with in regional Arab and African affairs. Its aspiration to regional military predominance has had the added effect of further increasing its domestic standing among elites and masses alike.

The *administrative* elite constitutes a second important component of the Algerian technocratic system. In fact, it is no exaggeration to say that with the increasing industrialization and complexity of Algerian society, the administrative stratum may soon replace the military as the paramount elite force.

This category includes the civil service, whose activities extend beyond the actual administration of the country into the substantive functions of various other ministries and their local networks. Included as well is a more narrowly defined new class of technocrats who have the authority and responsibility for the planning, development, operation, and expansion of the nation's industrial complex, particularly the petrochemical central base. In the process of nationalizing and socializing the petroleum and natural gas industries, numerous national companies (state monopolies) have been established with the most important being the oil empire, SONATRACH. The technical administrators of these companies have become the most important technocrats.

There are, in addition, economic technocrats included in the administrative elite—namely, the economic and financial planners and managers for the government-owned and government-operated banks, insurance companies, import and export controls, and related commercial activities.

This administrative elite has expanded enormously since the Boumediene takeover so that it has tended to break down into component groups. In fact, ever since the technocratic predominance began in the late 1960s, bureaucratic politics within the ministerial and presidential councils have been largely conducted among the leaders of technician subgroups. This administrative group constitutes an important subelite within the larger administrative elite and has been the most noticeable recipient of new class status including conspicuous wealth and other tangible signs of social advantage.

Unlike the other two technocratic elite groups of the military and the party, "the bureaucrats are a highly productive elite with a real impact on the country's development and hence, on the production of new elites. Whether it is the school, the factory, or the local assembly, the policy output of the administration creates new skills, new opportunities, new demands, and new sources of power. . . ." [Zartman, 1975:277]

While the role of the National Liberation Front (FLN) in the achievement of national independence was a decisive one, the FLN did not manage to maintain its power and prestige after independence. The factionalism that had been suppressed in the name of national unity during the revolution quickly reappeared as the *party* leaders vied with one another for positions of power. The quality of FLN leadership at the local level declined, and individual party officials in many cases seemed more intent on personal advancement than in building up the party as an effective peacetime organization.

As a consequence, the FLN has not been a very credible force in stimulating political activity or in mobilizing the masses. The heavy hands of the state and the army have not allowed it any independent political activity. It is unattractive to young people with an educated and intelligent interest in politics, since they are required as members to be more conformist than are nonmembers. Most debilitating has been the virtual powerlessness of the party which has been unable to dispense even the most minor favors and services. For the better part of Boumediene's rule, the FLN was anything but a vanguard party; instead its role was simply to propagate other's policy or defend others' candidates.

With all these shortcomings, however, the party retains a dominant position over all other national organizations while remaining distinctly inferior to the military and administrative elites. Even this subordinate status may soon change if the role provided for the FLN in the National Charter and constitution is in any way taken seriously. Part two of the charter for example, devotes a lengthy section to the "avant-garde" nature of the party which is to become the ideological vanguard of the socialist revolution. Moreover, political participation at any level of political organization requires FLN membership. All this reflects a desire to create a viable national political organization that will permit citizen participation in the political life of the state thereby decentralizing authority and enhancing the populist quality of the regime. Thus despite earlier predictions of the FLN's demise or, at best, its sustained insignificance, the party elites have now been given new responsibilities, power, and resources that may yet transform Algeria into an effective single-party system. As Boumediene told an assembly of mayors back in early 1973 when he initiated his campaign to reactivate party life: "A revolution needs revoluntionaries and the socialist revolution socialist militants. Whoever has faith in the revolution and its objectives must join the party. Otherwise he can have no place at any level of responsibility." Boumediene's immediate successors seemed to have taken his words to heart.

The various other national organizations including the workers union (*L'Union Générale des Travailleurs Algériens* or UGTA), farmers organization (*L'Union Nationale des Paysans Algériens* or UNPA), the Youth Association (*L'Union Nationale de la Jeunesse Algérienne* or UNJA), the organization of former *mujahidin* (*L'Organisation Nationale des Moudjahidine* or ONM), and the women's association (*L'Union Nationale des Femmes Algériennes* or UNFA), are all subordinate to the party with little or no independent power or authority. The only group that sought to challenge centralized authority and assert its own view, the student union (*L'Union Nationale des Etudiants Algériens* or UNEA, formerly known in the pre-1963 period as *L'Union Générale des Etudiants Musulmans d'Algérie* or UGEMA), was finally suppressed in the 1970s after a series of student boycotts, strikes, and demonstrations. It has not been revived since and is conspicuously absent from the list of national organizations included in the party section of the National Charter.

POLITICAL ECONOMY

More so than most countries, the Algerian economy is a matter of politics. This is only partly due to geography and history which have combined to give the economy its political character; more influential has been the deliberate decisions of Algeria's technocratic elites to bring the economy within the direction of the state.

In the decade following independence Algeria proceeded to nationalize all major foreign business interests as well as many private Algerian companies. Nationalization ranged from the assumption of a controlling interest in certain cases to complete takeover in others. Today the Algerian economy is almost totally government-controlled with the central government entirely responsible for economic planning, development, and administration. State enterprises and government agencies control much of the foreign trade, almost all of the major industries, large parts of the distribution and retail systems, all public utilities, and the entire banking and credit system.

The commitment to what has come to be called state capitalism evolved out of the radical nationalism of the Boumediene group. The realization of true national independence came to be defined in terms of control of natural resources, especially hydro-carbons, and rapid industrial development—objectives which, in the context of world capitalist domination, could only be achieved through nationalization and state control of the economy.

Since the late 1960s, the economic strategy of the technocratic elite has been to give priority to industrial over agricultural development and, within the industrial sector, to basic industries so as to produce an accelerator effect, bringing the creation of secondary industries in their wake. The regime's deliberate decision to slight the needs of agriculture and the rural population in favor of rapid industrialization and in favor of the urban-based programs of higher education and advanced technical training needed to staff an industrializing economy has been based on two arguments.

First, the continued production of only raw materials and agricultural products for export would not have enabled Algeria to achieve the kind of economic independence deemed necessary to make political independence truly meaningful, while the impossibility of rapidly improving agricultural pro-· ductivity without industrial support would have kept the country permanently backward and in debt. In addition, Algeria's abundant supply of hydrocarbons ensure rapid capital accumulation through the capital its export would bring in and could serve as the base of heavy industry.

The subsequent huge differentials in investment between agriculture and industry were explained by the argument that agriculture was already an ongoing sector whereas industry had to be built from practically nothing. In any case, the rural population of Algeria could not be supported at a reasonable standard of living on the limited agricultural land available and must therefore find employment in industry. Industry, in turn, will provide machinery and fertilizers for agriculture as well as furnishing a market for an improved and increased agricultural output. To this is added the government's belief that in the course of time, industrialization will lead to the creation of new jobs on a large scale, thereby somewhat offsetting the chronic problem of unemployment and underemployment in the countryside (estimated as high as 60 percent) and in the cities (20 percent). In the short run, however, employment generated by the new capital-intensive industries cannot more than marginally alleviate the unemployment problem, especially in the context of one of the world's highest population growth rates. This is why since November 1971, when the "Charter of the Agrarian

Revolution" was proclaimed with the intent of profoundly changing the economic and political cast of the traditional sector of Algerian agriculture, there has been a gradual correcting of the severe investment imbalance between the industrial and agricultural sectors. A comparison of the regime's two four-year development plans demonstrates this policy shift.

The first four-year plan (1970–1973) marked the first real effort at a global economic policy. The plan emphasized the establishment of a capital-intensive sector, involving the hydrocarbon, iron and steel, chemical and engineering industries, which was to serve as a basis for economic growth. The plan allocated 45 percent of investments to industry, 15 percent to agriculture, and 40 percent to social and economic infrastructure. The favored position of the industrial sector and public works vis-à-vis agriculture reflected Algeria's policy of "planting her oil" and thereby using its returns to create an organized and interrelated industrial structure. The Agrarian revolution policy aimed at improving efficiency through land reform, but a system of cooperatives failed to improve agriculture's percentage of GNP which, in fact, declined from 13 percent in 1969, to 9 percent in 1973.

The second four year plan (1974–1977) aimed at remedying the apparent imbalances and malfunctions of the first plan without, however, jeapordizing the absolute preponderance of industry or the high rate of investment. While still paying attention to the heavy industry base, the new plan has put more emphasis on developing consumer goods industries that create jobs, fighting against regional disparities, building up small and medium-sized industries throughout the country, and extending the agrarian revolution in order to give land to thousands of people actively working to stimulate national savings, and to reduce superfluous consumption. In addition, the 1974–1977 plan places a major emphasis on housing, an area that was conspicuously neglected in the first plan. A comparison of the investment patterns by sectors in both plans is indicated in Table 2.

It is yet uncertain how much of this new and major investment in agriculture will find its way into the improvement of the poorest parts of the countryside, as opposed to the state and self-managed farms, and more particularly how much success the authorities will have in coping with what are, in fact, very intractable problems in transforming the conditions of rural life. Besides money, of course, what is needed are qualified personnel, education, and effective means of inducing social and cultural changes in the life habits of the peasant population.

Algeria's industrial development and commiment to massive industrialization has been made possible by the country's large petroleum production and potentially enormous natural gas production. The petroleum industry, begun by French companies during the revolutionary war and continued by them thereafter under the terms of the Evian Accords of 1962, progressively came under greater Algerian control with subsequent agreements negotiated in 1965 and 1971. By 1971, Algeria acquired a majority interest in the production, refining, and transportation of her oil and a monopoly of internal distribution. Meanwhile, the foreign exchange she derived from oil exports, which in 1969 stood at only US $250 million, reached $5 billion in 1974, thanks to the great worldwide price increase of 1973. While her proven reserves are limited, and in 1971 it was estimated that they would suffice for only another thirty years' production at current rates, the current and prospective income has already dramatically revolutionized her opportunities for investment in general national economic growth. Thus already in 1973, before most of the impact of that year's price rise had been felt, the petroleum sector accounted for over 75 percent of Algeria's exports, 68 percent of her foreign ex-

TABLE 2

Algerian General Investment Structure, 1967–1977

(in millions of Algerian Dinars)

	1967–1969	Four-Year Plan (1970–1973) Estimates	Four-Year Plan Realization	Second Four-Year Plan (1974–1977) Estimates
Agriculture	1,606	4,140	4,990.5	12,005
Industry	4,750	12,500	17,653.4	48,000
Transports	—	800	793.4	—
Tourism	177	700	700.0	1,200
Infrastructure	855	2,307	2,024.3	15,521
Education and Training	870	3,307	2,982.3	9,947
Housing	249	1,520	1,614.9	15,600
Public Services and Administration	533	2,566	2,564.0	—

SOURCE: Jean Leca, "Algerian Socialism: Nationalism, Industrialization, and State-Building," in *Socialism in the Third World*, ed. Helen Desfosses and Jacques Levesque (New York: Praeger Publishers, 1975), p. 145, Table I.

change earnings, and 35 percent of the government's budget revenues. Gross domestic product, which had risen by 10 percent per year from 1969 to 1972, and over 18 perecnt in 1973 alone, reached $6 billion in the latter year.

The program of industrialization centers naturally around projects related to oil and gas: refining, gas liquification, pipelines, port facilities, tankers, petrochemicals, fertilizers, synthetic rubber, artificial fibers, and plastics. Four refineries are in current operation. Gas liquification plants at Arzew and Skikda will be supplemented by others. An iron and steel complex near Annaba is in operation capitalizing on substantial iron ore deposits in the northeast; in addition, a very large deposit of ore, estimated at 2 billion tons, is located at Tindouf near the Moroccan and Mauritanian borders [Kerr, 1976:397–98].

Ironically, what was initially a peasant revolution has culminated in a form of vigorous state capitalism, utilizing both modern large-scale techniques and small-scale local plants. In addition, industrialization has tended to bifurcate society into isolated poles of growth and stagnation which will take more than money or good will to overcome. Finally, Algeria's state capitalism has created and sustained a new elite. This economic system has put a premium on centralized control of the whole economy and on nationalization of the means of production. Thus economic power is concentrated in the hands of the state officials who run the central national enterprises. Technical efficiency and material productivity have become the prime objectives of development, and success is judged in terms of profits. Those state capitalists who are the most efficient, technically competent, and profit-motivated individuals have risen to the status of technocrat elite who, in time, may become the new rulers of Algerian society.

FOREIGN POLICY

Algerian foreign policy has been strongly influenced by the revolutionary experience of the nearly eight-year war of independence, an experience which has left a legacy of emotional extremism, verbal excess, and diplomatic abrasiveness in the conduct of foreign affairs. Policy is further affected by the Algerian predisposition to suspicion inherent in the political culture but further nurtured by a clandestine guerrilla life and the internal rivalries of postindependence politics. It is thus through analogy with Algeria's revolutionary experiences, problems, and solutions and the particular cultural configuration of its own domestic socializing processes that the country's view of foreign affairs has been shaped.

Despite the country's modest natural and human resources and limited military capabilities, Algeria sees itself as playing a major role in world politics. In geopolitical terms the country's leaders have described Algeria as the "core" state of the Maghrib, on the borders of the Mediterranean, with a dual attachment to the African and Arab worlds and thus ideally placed to be at the crossroads of three continents. In the important context of international political economy, Algeria has taken a leading role in the relationship between the producers of energy, industrialized consumers, and the developing countries of the Third World. Algerian nationalization of its own oil industry and the policies it has been able to pursue as part of the OPEC cartel are the most important ways in which Algeria has sought to be an exemplar to the rest of the Third World.

Emotionally and ideologically, Algeria's strong commitment to revolutionary freedom has brought it into spiritual communion with those nations it has felt have undergone a similar experience, notably Yugoslavia, Cuba, and Vietnam. One practical consequence of this revolutionary ardor has been the emergence of Algiers as a center for any number of black African liberation movements, and even of fringe revolutionary groups in Latin America, the Middle East, and other parts of the world. In recent years, however, it has tended to discourage revolutionary "renegades" such as America's Black Panther Party from establishing a political presence in the capital. In fact, unlike Ben Bella, Boumediene and now Chadli have reduced verbal encouragement for violent revolutionary activities especially where these may jeoparidze advantageous economic relationships. Yet given the Arab-oriented background of the Algerian president and the mythology of the success of the revolution—an exaggeration and distortion being continually shaped by current leaders into a central pillar of the new national tradition—certain dominant principles of foreign policy have remained throughout the postindependence period: namely, nonalignment in the global struggle between the two superpowers, identification with the Third World, promotion of revolutionary independence movements and wars of national liberation directed at colonialism and imperialism, advocacy of African and Arab unity, and unswerving suppport for the Palestinian cause in its struggle against Israel and Zionism.

Given such an orientation—although more radical in words than deeds—it was inevitable that Algeria would come into conflict with its immediate neighbors to the east and west. With Morocco, for example, there have been serious disagreements involving border and ideological issues leading to direct armed conflict in 1963 and indirect military engagement via the Algerian-supported Polisario Front in 1976 and 1977. Should the dispute over Morocco's annexation of the northern two-thirds of former Spanish Sahara, an area that Algeria would like to see become independent, be eventually resolved there would still remain serious disagreement given the fundamental dissonance in attitude, style, and ultimate objectives between the two countries.

The situation is somewhat more favorable concerning Tunisia, where territorial disputes have been resolved in favor of Algeria and its petroleum and gas interests. Yet here too, Bourguiba's espousal of Western values and Tunisia's particularly warm and close relationships with France and the United States makes it ultimately suspect by the more cautious Algerian decision-makers.

Yet neither territorial nor ideological differences have permanently alienated Algeria from Tunisia and Morocco, notwithstanding the severing of diplomatic relations with the latter over the Spanish Sahara issue. This then constitutes one of the outstanding features of Algerian foreign policy: despite its revolutionary rhetoric, austere manner, and radical posturing, Algeria maintains direct and continuing contacts with a wide variety of different regimes qualifying it as one of the few countries in the world to advocate and successfully maintain a truly nonaligned position in international affairs. Thus not only was Algeria virtually the only party capable of successfully mediating between Libya and Egypt in their recent (summer 1977), bloody border skirmish, but it has been able to sustain a close military assistance relationship with the Soviet Union—the latter supplying planes, tanks, and other arms to Algeria, training cadets for the officer corps, and supplying several thousand technicians—while simultaneously developing an extensive economic relationship with the United States. In fact, in 1976 the United States became Algeria's main trading partner, supplanting France in that position. France still maintains particular advantage in Algerian bilateral relations given the extensive economic, cultural, and trading ties that exist; yet even this close involvement has not compromised Algeria's independence of outside powers. This in itself is a remarkable achievement given the condition of structural dependency that inhibits the full development of many former colonial states of the Third World.

Under Boumediene Algeria has been able to maintain its call for Third World liberation while being in the forefront of those oil-producing states seeking to coordinate Third World economic policy vis-à-vis the Western industrial nations in accordance with lessons learned from Arab oil-embargo policies. Foreign policy rhetoric, however, is never allowed to interfere with foreign trade dealings and international business transactions which Algeria conducts in a highly business-like and efficient manner, all seemingly designed to let others understand that its commerce and its foreign policy rhetoric are quite distinct matters.

TUNISIA

POSTINDEPENDENCE POLITICS

THE HISTORY OF POSTINDEPENDENCE POLITICS in Tunisia has been dominated by two overwhelming forces: the charismatic personality and popular appeal of Habib Bourguiba, the country's only president in twenty years of independence, and the political supremacy of the Destourian Socialist Party (*Parti Socialiste Destourien* or PSD) over all other national organizations and governmental institutions. In a typically immodest yet accurate response to a journalist's query about the Tunisian political system, Bourguiba once stated: "What system? I *am* the system." Despite the increasingly authoritarian cast that Tunisian political life has assumed in recent years, the role of the indefatigable "Supreme Warrior" has been instrumental in providing the needed national unity and political stability to a country that remains inherently vulnerable to disequilibrium given its meager socioeconomic resources, its military inferiority vis-à-vis some of its more powerful Arab and African neighbors, the persistence of social, regional, and ideological cleavages, and the debilitating impact of over seventy years of French colonial rule. Indeed, it is not exaggeration to credit Bourguiba's authoritarian presence and manipulative skills for allowing Tunisia to evolve over the years into a relatively stable, effective, and developed polity.

The tactics and approaches used so successfully by the preindependence nationalist elites and subsequent governing class during an earlier period, however, may no longer be relevant or productive in a later period of development. This, in fact, constitutes the system's severest challenge in the 1980s: are the men, institutions, and policies that successfully guided Tunisia to independence and established its political direction in the decade thereafter still relevant to a younger generation of men and women who are less awed by the preindependence struggle or psychologically ravished by the colonialist experience and whose contemporary political beliefs and socioeconomic priorities differ markedly from their elders in power? In addition, does the system created by Bourguiba and his contemporaries possess sufficient legitimacy and adaptability to respond to the simultaneous pressures for social change and justice, economic growth and development, and political participation and equality made by an increasingly articulate and vocal segment of the country's newly educated young? To date the record has been uneven as Bourguiba's Tunisia has alternated between reconciliation and mobilization systems of rule and development depending on how threats and challenges to the regime have been perceived by the incumbent elite. A reconciliation system is one which adopts the methods of mediation between conflicting interests, balancing contradictory proposals and recommendations, and persuading opposing groups to act in harmony in order to achieve development. A mobilization system, on the other hand, uses techniques of mass mobilization, propaganda, coercion, and sophisticated organization to achieve the goals of political and socioeconomic development.

Five analytically distinct yet empirically overlapping historical phases reflecting these alternating strategies are identifiable in postindependence Tunisia: Phase I, 1955–1959, when Bourguiba successfully fought off internal opposition and consolidated his power via the strong support of the Neo-Destour Party; Phase II, 1960–1963, a transitional stage marked by a gradual shift from a reconciliatory policy to more state control of development; Phase III, 1964–1969, a mobilizational period highlighted by the rise and precipitous fall of Ahmad Ben Salah and his socialist cooperativist scheme; Phase IV, 1970–1974, when both political and economic life were one again liberalized, at least at the elite level, only to be overturned shortly thereafter; Phase V, 1975 to the present, the latest stage of Bourguibist rule with increasing authoritarian tendencies in the political sphere and greater reliance on capitalist support in the form of accelerated foreign investments and encouragement of private enterprise domestically as a counter to previously articulated socialist goals and policies. This latter mobilizational phase has aroused strong oppositional tendencies among a relatively small but extremely vocal group of liberal politicians, leftist university students, intellectuals, and activist labor leaders.

PHASE I: 1955–1959—INTERNAL SPLITS AND CONSOLIDATION OF POWER

The short transition period between the June 3, 1955, signing of a convention between France and Tunisia proclaiming the latter's internal autonomy and full independence on March 20, 1956, in the form of a Franco-Tunisian protocol abrogating the 1881 Treaty of Bardo and giving Tunisia complete political sovereignty as a monarchy was marked by an internal split in the nationalist Neo-Destour Party. The secretary-general of the party, Salah Ben Youssef, who had been in Cairo since 1952, returned to Tunisia in September 1955, three months after Bourguiba's own triumphant return from three years of exile. Denouncing the autonomy convention with France as a "step backward," Ben Youssef openly attacked Bourguiba and called instead for immediate Tunisian independence within the framework of Pan-Arab advancement. Towards this end he had the popular support of strongly religious and conservative groups as well as urban elements that sympathized with Ben Youssef's brand of radical Arab nationalism which drew ideological inspiration from Nasserism in Egypt. Bourguiba, on the other hand, represented moderation, an attachment to specifically Tunisian as opposed to Arab-Islamic virtures and possibilities, and had the support of educated, gallicized, western-trained elites from the Sahel and Tunis, that is, from society's more modernized sector.

In the bitter and personal confrontation that took place between these two charismatic personalities, Bourguiba was able to prevail with the unanimous support of the party and the crucial backing of the trade union movement, headed by Bourguiba's ally, Ahmad Ben Salah. In October 1955, Ben Youssef was expelled from the party and a month later, at the Neo-Destour's fifth party congress in Sfax, the expulsion was confirmed and Bourguiba reelected as party president. The party congress also reaffirmed its commitment to total independence as a national goal and significantly added resolutions supporting the struggles for freedom of the Moroccan and Algerian peoples.

These actions did not overcome the bitterness felt by Ben Youssef supporters but instead led to clashes between Bourguibist and Youssefist factions. In December 1955, a conspiracy to set up and direct terrorist *fellagha* groups in the south as a means by which to prevent the implementation of the Franco-Tunisian agreement was discovered. Salah Ben Youssef fled to Libya in January 1956, and many suspected Youssefists were placed in detention. This did not stop *fellagha* activity and terrorism directed at both Frenchmen and Neo-Destour members from continuing, although the independence negotiations that began in Paris on February 27, 1956, between the Bourguiba-led Tunisian delegation and the French government virtually eliminated Youssefism as a threat to Tunisian independence.

Although defeated politically and then militarily, Youssefism surfaced again in a plot against Bourguiba in 1962, a year after the assassination of its leader in Frankfurt, Germany. At that time the Youssefists, along with military malcontents, were reacting against the costly failure of Bourguiba's Bizerte policy the year before. Salah Ben Youssef, Youssefism, and neo-Youssefism (the latter used to refer to those who continued to support the ideas of radical Pan-Arabism, Islamic beliefs and practices, socialism, and anti-Westernism) all constituted the most severe direct political and military domestic challenge confronting Bourguiba and the Neo-Destour. More important, perhaps, was the fact that Youssefism and its challenge to Bourguiba's rule had far-reaching effects on the future course of the regime and shifted it permanently onto authoritarian ground, fixing the style of Bourguiba's power.

The termination of the Youssefist split and the granting of political independence in March 1956, did not completely eliminate internal differences as a conflict between Bourguiba and his former supporter, Ben Salah, subsequently emerged. Essentially, Bourguiba's political objectives were to unify the party on the broadest possible base, to secure a virtual monopoly for it, and not to risk national unity or foreign investment by radical economic change. Ben Salah, on the other hand, envisioned the General Union of Tunisian Workers *(Union Générale des Travailleurs Tunisiens* or UGTT)* as the national instrument for social and economic revolution. He also spoke of the nationalization of all resources and proclaimed the need for a socialist plan for development. The disruption of the policy of gradualism and the bid for the union movement for direct social and economic policy were all unacceptable to Bourguiba. Exploiting existing rivalries within the UGTT, Bourguiba in December 1956, was eventually able to have Ben Salah removed as head of the union and replaced by Ahmed Tlili who shared Bourguiba's vision of a liberal, reformist system of social and economic change.

Thus in the first years of autonomy and independence, Bourguiba was able to establish his supremacy not only in the party but also in the formal machinery of the state. Elections for a constituent assembly, for example, were held merely five days after independence with all ninety-eight seats being won by National Front candidates, all of whom acknowledged allegiance to the Neo-Destour. Habib Bourguiba became prime minister on April 11, leading a government in which sixteen of the seventeen ministers belonged to the Neo-Destour.

The first official act of the assembly, on July 25, 1957, was to pass a unanimous resolution abolishing the powerless and unpopular position of the *bey* or monarchy and proclaiming Tunisia a republic. Bourguiba was made provisional "President of the Republic" and given the *bey*'s full executive and legislative powers until the assembly could produce a constitution.

The salient characteristic of the two-year transitional period prior to the November 1959 general elections was the concentration of power in the hands of the president and his cabinet. It is significant that the most important and striking reform legislation enacted during the entire independent period came through presidential decree and without legislative review in the period between 1956 and 1959.

The Constituent Assembly finally approved the draft constitution on June 1, 1959, which was ratified and promulgated on the same date by President Bourguiba. The new constitution established Tunisia as a republican state, with Islam as its religion, and Arabic its language, which forms a part of the Greater Maghrib.

The 1959 constitution confirmed the authority of the president, particularly vis-à-vis the assembly. Both were to be elected at the same time for a period of five years with the president limited to three consecutive terms. But the government was made responsible to the president, not to the assembly, and the latter was limited to meeting for six months of the year. The system which thus emerged was that of a "presidential monarchy" with Bourguiba taking over the position of the *bey* while at the same time remaining at the head of an effective political party.

On November 8, 1959, Tunisia held its first elections under the new constitution. President Bourguiba ran unopposed, and assembly candidates, backed by the Neo-Destour and affiliated labor and professional groups, had only token opposition.

Thus by the end of 1959, Habib Bourguiba and his Neo-Destour Party had placed their indelible imprint on the Tunisian political system. Independence had been achieved with little bloodshed or cost; the man and his party were universally acknowledged as the direct instruments for independence with their political power fully legitimized; the serious split with Ben Youssef was successfully overcome as was Ahmad Ben Salah's secondary challenge in the UGTT; and the structural and institutional framework of republican Tunisia was put into place with the promulgation of the 1959 constitution and the subsequent legislative and presidential elections won by the Neo-Destour—all ninety assembly seats—and Habib Bourguiba.

PHASE II: 1960–1964—PERIOD OF TRANSITION

A series of internal and external crises along with the regime's gradual shift from a previous dependence on private entrepreneurship for economic modernization to a policy based on systematic planning highlighted the second phase of political evolution.

In July 1961, Tunisia became embroiled in the Bizerte crisis involving Tunisian demands for the complete evacuation of French naval and military presence in the port of Bizerte. Excessive French military reaction involving the attack of Bizerte and the subsequent death of hundreds of Tunisian civilians aroused international anger and, reminiscent of the 1956 Suez invasion by Anglo-French forces, led to universal condemnation of French actions while simultaneously enhancing the prestige and popularity of Bourguiba in the eyes of his own people and the world community.

This did not stop Youssefist supporters, however, from hatching an assassination plot against Bourguiba, who undoubtedly was behind the "mysterious" murder of Ben Youssef in a Frankfurt hotel in August 1961. In any case, the assassination plot was discovered in December 1962, and several junior army officers, including former officers in the *bey*'s forces, a member of the Presidential Guard, and a former commander of the armored forces, were arrested, convicted, and executed. The Communist Party was banned, and Tunisian-Algerian relations were suspended in the aftermath of this affair.

Rather than undermining Bourguiba's power, both these events strengthened his position at home and abroad and further allowed the expansion of his authoritarian system of rule. It was in the economic realm that Bourguiba's policies seemed noticeably inadequate, however. In fact, the policies pursued in the first half decade of independence proved unsuccessful in either attracting significant private investment or preventing a collapse in the economy. By adopting systematic planning, the ruling elite intended to encourage economic growth, to break up the rigidities of social stratification, to equalize opportunities, and to increase social mobility. Towards this end, in May 1964, the Tunisian National Assembly enacted legislation authorizing the expropriation of all foreign-owned lands, mostly French.

The nationalization legislation marked a significant step towards the development of socialism in the agrarian sector of the economy and reflected the regime's shift towards a more mobilizational orientation. At the October 1964 congress of the Neo-Destour held in Bizerte, the party's name was officially changed to the "Destourian Socialist Party" so as to emphasize the party's commitment to Tunisian socialism.

The second phase comes to an end with the presidential and legislative elections of November 8, 1964, in which Bourguiba was again elected president unopposed and the PSD, the only party to present candidates, filled all seats in the National Assembly. The transitional period thus witnessed the further institutionalization of Bourguibist rule with a gradual moving away from a free-enterprise system in the economic sphere and a greater reliance on mobilizational techniques in the political sphere.

PHASE III: 1964–1969—RISE AND FALL OF SOCIALISM

Between 1964 and 1969 the chief issue dominating internal politics was the drive to collectivize agriculture, carried out under the leadership of Ahmad Ben Salah, the influential minister of finance and planning who was brought back into government in 1961 after a five year absence. With the full support of Bourguiba and the party, Ben Salah proceeded to develop a wide-ranging and ambitious ten-year plan of economic development and reform based almost completely on state control and initiative in industry and agriculture. At the 1964 party congress, this ten-year plan was formally adopted with the enthusiastic support of Bourguiba himself. And, as noted, the party's name change was undertaken to demonstrate complete commitment to the plan's socialist objectives.

Ben Salah was committed to developing a new, cooperative sector of the economy although he made very few adjustments of an institutional nature in executing his developmental plan. The core of Ben Salah's scheme was the system of agricultural cooperatives that were to be developed on the large nationalized French estates in the north of the country but also involving the participation of Tunisian smallholders as well.

In spite of the merits of Ben Salah's policies, they began to meet increasing resistance especially in the countryside where small landowners and landless peasants alike found their wishes ignored and their needs misunderstood. When Ben Salah's cooperative scheme extended beyond the former French-dominated regions into the Sahel and threatened the status of larger Tunisian landowners, many of whom possessed personal ties in Tunis and the government, opposition to Ben Salah became more directly political. In Ben Salah's hands the cooperative organizations began to rival the scope and effectiveness of the PSD itself. By early 1969, the cooperatives for agriculture included and affected roughly one-third of the active rural population, and nearly all industrial and commercial activities in the cities were affected by their activities. Inevitably, Ben Salah's mismanagement, which resulted in large sums having to be pumped as subsidies into an increasingly unproductive agriculture, the failure of other portions of the development plan, and the threatening nature of Ben Salah's centralized power led, in September 1969, to his dismissal as secretary of state for planning and the national economy and later, in May 1970, to his imprisonment to ten years' hard labor on assorted charges of financial mismanagement, abuses, mistakes, and irregularities. He was later to escape in February 1973, and take refuge in Europe. More importantly, the regime scrapped Ben Salah's agricultural policies and abandoned most of the socialist orientation he had introduced to the nation's economic policy-making.

The Ben Salah affair and the radical socialist objectives associated with it represented the second most serious challenge that Bourguiba has had to face since the threat of Youssefism in the middle 1950s. Bourguiba was indirectly implicated because of the political support and the warm personal encouragement he had earlier given to Ben Salah. As a consequence, the president's prestige and popularity suffered severely offset only by public sympathy for Bourguiba's chronic illness and weakened physical state which resulted in prolonged absences abroad for medical treatment.

The president's political popularity and control of the party and government, however, remained unchallenged as reflected in the November 2, 1969, presidential and National Assembly elections. Bourguiba was reelected for a third term and all seats for the National Assembly were won by members of the PSD.

PHASE IV: 1970–1974—LIBERALISM (TEMPORARILY) REVIVED

Following the disastrous period of socialist experimentation and the uncertain health of the country's leader, there emerged a springtime of liberalism as Bourguiba sought to reassert his authority, stabilize the system, and advance its economy. Several former high government officials who had been turned out of power in the heyday of Ben Salah's expansive authority were reintegrated into important positions in the party and government. Thus Ahmed Mestiri, who had resigned as secretary of state for defense in opposition to the excessive speed of the policy of cooperatives, was brought back into the party and government in 1970; Habib Achour was once again made head of the UGTT; Bahi Ladgham was appointed prime minister and, when asked to serve as an arbiter between Jordan's King Hussein and the Palestinians, was replaced by Bourguiba's close ally and respected politician, Hedi Nouira in November 1970.

The government's greater sensitivity to charges of excessive zeal and authoritarian tendencies as exhibited during the Ben Salah period was no better revealed than at the 1971 PSD congress held in Bourguiba's birthplace of Monastir in the Sahel. The characteristic balance between authoritarianism and liberalism evident in the regime tipped decisively towards liberalism and reconciliation at Monastir. Discussion was free and open, democratic in spirit and practice. Policy alternatives were heatedly debated and past mistakes acknowledged. Most importantly, Bourguiba did not impose his point of view but rather allowed the party to serve as a genuine articulator and aggregator of diverse political and social interests.

Yet in the key political positions, such as appointments to the PSD's ruling political bureau, Bourguiba maintained his unchallenged authority, choosing his hand-picked men while ignoring the results of party elections to the Political Bureau and Central Committee which favored increased liberalism and competitive politics as represented by such men as Ahmed Mestiri.

Over the next three years the hopes of liberalism were gradually eliminated as both Bourguiba's personal health and political stamina bounced back with ever greater vigor. At the September 1974 ninth PSD congress, for example, held once again in Monastir, Bourguiba announced that "it was necessary to eradicate what happened in the last congress." The congress delegates unanimously acclaimed Bourguiba as party president for life and called for a constitutional amendment to make him president-for-life of the republic. The delegates also erased the 1971 decision by which the sixty-man Central Committee elected by the congress would in turn elect a Political Bureau, the party's highest body. The congress reestablished the system by which the president named the bureau's members. In short, Bourguiba had reasserted and consolidated his control over the party extinguishing in the process any hope for a more liberalized, competitive party system.

On November 3, 1974, Bourguiba was reelected unopposed to a fourth consecutive term as president. All 112 seats of the newly enlarged National Assembly were competed for by PSD candidates. A month later, on December 17, 1974, the new National Assembly voted by acclamation to amend article 40 of the constitution to permit Bourguiba to remain president for life "as an exceptional measure and in recognition of services rendered." The measuer made the premier, Hedi Nouira in this case, the automatic successor in the event of the president's death or incapacity.

The years 1970–1974 thus witnessed the rise and rapid decline of a liberal spirit in Tunisian politics. The expectation that possibly a two-party system would eventually emerge reflecting Tunisia's increasing political sophistication and development was emphatically turned back by Bourguiba and his party deputies. To insure that opposition trends of any kind did not emerge, the state began to employ greater and greater amounts of coercive force especially against dissident university students who reacted violently in virtually yearly demonstrations, beginning as early as 1965, against the regime's authoritarianism and repressive policies. While basic political order had been maintained and mass popular support continued, especially in the countryside, authority was increasingly dependent on coercive rather than legitimate force.

PHASE V: 1975 TO THE PRESENT—POLITICAL AUTHORITARIANISM AND A FREE ENTERPRISE ECONOMY

As the political system has become more and more closed, the economic system has become increasingly open. Not only have former and current opposition figures and dissident groups been effectively removed from the political process, but even the PSD itself has virtually collapsed as a single party of any political consequence. In certain respects the presidential monarchy is beginning to resemble King Hassan's Morocco. Personal power has in both cases eroded political infrastructure, and Destourian socialism has been reinterpreted to mean a liberalization of the economy. In making his political comeback after 1969 and more so since 1974, Bourguiba has once and for all destroyed the party as a living infrastructure which might accommodate the various factions persisting in the national political arena. The PSD today simply functions to orchestrate the adulation of the leader.

Yet the opposition has not remained silent. In March 1976, for example, a group headed by former Interior Minister Mestiri issued a declaration which said that the one-party system was "no longer adapted to the needs and aspirations of the people" and called for an organized opposition outside of the PSD. Over a year later in June 1977, a National Council for the Defense of Public Liberties was formed, bringing together the broadest possible coalition—from extreme leftists to supporters of pan-Islamic integration—under the label of "social democrats," whose single common denominator was the desire to create a pluralist democracy based on the respect for public liberties and human rights. While this may not constitute the "organized opposition" Mestiri's group called for, it does represent a continuing trend against the pervasive authoritarianism that has become Bourguiba's Tunisia.

A more forceful oppositional group has been the well-organized trade union movement (UGTT) which in January 1978, organized a general strike, the first in the history of independent Tunisia. Union supporters, including *lycée* and university students in large numbers, and government military and police forces clashed violently following several months of labor unrest. The general strike and conflict left numerous dead and wounded, resulting in convictions for twenty-four union leaders including the popular Habib

Achour, ranging up to ten years at hard labor for harming
the internal security of the country. Clearly the large number
of convictions (over 300), as well as the number of deaths
(estimated between 50 and 200) and injuries indicated the
existence of a relatively powerful opposition group. Both the
widespread participation of labor members and students and
the use of the military to restore law and order revealed the
regime's political fragility and ever-decreasing legitimacy.
Yet within six short months the government had effectively
crushed the opposition and reestablished the supremacy of
the Bourguibist system. Nonetheless, the future is none too
promising given the history of violent opposition among
society's key labor, student, and intellectual sectors.

Economically, Prime Minister Hedi Nouira, who has been
in that position since 1970 and now virtually runs the government as Bourguiba appears in ill-health, has put an end to
moves toward socialism, loosened controls on business and
industry, and encouraged private Tunisian and foreign investment. The results have been mixed, yet the regime now appears committed to a policy of "opening up" to foreign investment and private enterprise; an economic policy which is
making Tunisia resemble more and more Sadat's Egypt with
its "open door" policy.

While Nouira has proved his skill as a manager, he has
failed to unite the PSD behind him. Lacking Bourguiba's
prestige, charisma, and political capacity, he seems unable
to cope with the splits and rivalries among the political clans.
As party secretary general, he has shown little tolerance for
opposition and is unlikely to win an election.

POLITICAL CULTURE AND IDEOLOGY

At the core of the Bourguibist system has been its stress on
cultural modernity, humanistic transformation, ideological

change, and social adaptation according to a gallicized model of progressive development and modernization. The ruling elite are conscious and proud of what they call Tunisia's Mediterranean heritage, which draws historical inspiration from Carthage and Rome, and from Arab and European cultures. Even more than their counterparts in Algeria and Morocco, the Tunisian elite identify deeply and intimately with French language, culture, and civilization. Bourguiba has long placed emphasis on Mediterranean Islam and the Franco-Tunisian systhesis as the core around which Tunisia's dominant political culture is to evolve. Despite pressures from traditional elements and supporters of Arabization and Islamization, the dominant elite have continued to pursue a policy of biculturalism and bilingualism. In this way they hope to effect a cultural posture that is equally amenable to Arab and Western civilizations.

In speaking about ideology and the role of political belief system in the developmental process in Tunisia, it is instructive to refer to the broader phenomenon as it applies to the Maghrib and the Middle East. In terms of its relationship to the processes of modernization, political development, and social change, ideology in the modern Arab world may be broken down into three distinct categories: radical, reactionary, and reformist.

Radical ideology encompasses the whole spectrum of strongly populist, transnationalist, anti-Western, socialist, centralist, and revolutionary tendencies that have surfaced and proliferated in the area since the first Arab defeat in the 1948 Palestine war. Representative examples include, *inter alia,* Pan-Arabism, Ba'athism, neo-Nasserism, and Arab socialism as well as the "imported" ideologies in evidence both before and since the Palestine defeat such as communism, Maoism, and revolutionism.

While fulfilling numerous psychocultural and moral needs

of both individual Arabs and Arab national communities, in the modern period radical ideology has failed to translate national mythology into a practical framework for political organization and action. This is not to ignore Arab nationalism as a movement articulating an Arab definition of purpose, morality, salvation, immortality, and theodicy. But as a political belief system aimed at political action radical Arab ideology has been singularly unsuccessful. Radical ideology is more symbolic than real, more expressive than practical. While it enables competing and contrasting social sectors to identify with a common ideal and creates, if only temporarily, the kind of surface harmony required to carry out the edicts and policies of the revolutionary elite, it nevertheless impedes the development of durable political organization necessary for the eventual institutionalization of any political belief system. And in the absence of legitimate, enduring, and effective political structures, the multifaceted problems associated with the processes of political development and social change appear immune to even partial resolution.

In addition, while it speaks and acts in the name of the masses, radical ideology is essentially antihumanistic. It seeks to erase individual social consciousness in behalf of a larger collectivist effort and, in so doing, virtually eliminates individual identity, individual rights, and individual freedoms. Not infrequently, government-led attempts at social leveling and social engineering are justified in humanistic terms with an emphasis placed on the nonexploitive character of equalitarian human relationships. Nonetheless, in the short run at least, radical ideology is less concerned with individual human rights and liberties than with the goals of massive mobilization and materialistic modernization, however injurious this may be to the humanistic consciousness of individual citizens.

Islamic fundamentalist principles and other tradition-bound belief systems articulated by such groups as the Muslim Brotherhood (*al-Ikhwan al-Muslimin*) and the monarchical ruling elites in Saudi Arabia, Kuwait, Morocco, Jordan, and the microstates of the Persian Gulf area represent the reactionary dimension of contemporary Arab ideology. Reactionary ideology espouses and promotes a primitive Islamic world view based on fundamentalist tenets as expounded in Islamic religious law and teachings and from which norms of political conduct and behavior are established. Reactionary ideology is oriented towards an authoritarian policy of social change legitimized in tradition and religion.

By definition reactionary ideology is hostile to the scientific-exploratory perspective. Hence its predominance among the more "backward" sectors of Arab society notwithstanding the accidental confluence of reactionary ideology with certain modernizing structures created as the result of enormous oil wealth. While patrimonial political systems of this sort have created relatively modern bureaucracies, armies, and technological cadres and, in some instances, have adopted technical innovation, scientific education, and economic enterprises they have refused to allow changes in norms, values, political institutions and practices. The theocratic nature of reactionary ideology and the devoutly religious makeup of Islamic patrimonialism are at odds with modern man's attempt to resolve the crises of participation, integration, and legitimacy.

Reformist ideology constitutes the third of the major ideological orientations found in the Arab world today. Its characteristics include both the symbolic outputs identified with radical ideology as well as the practical components of realism, adaptability, accommodation, organization, and efficacity associated with conventional Western democratic systems. Like radical ideology, a reformist orientation seeks to reassure both articulator and audience, to engender solidarity, and to resolve problems of personal or group identity.

But reformism also systematically relates ideological goals to political means and creates appropriate organizational structures to institutionalize such relationships.

Whereas reactionary ideology reinforces the dominant traditional political culture and radical ideology postulates a world view only distantly related to the prevailing political culture, reformist ideology is lively and meaningful to the progressive and better educated. Reformist ideology puts a premium on human liberty and individual rights even under the unavoidably stressful conditions of modernization when political cohesion and social consensus are necessary to build and buttress a modern national community, The creation of "practical" organization committed to individual human rights seems essential if a humanistic as opposed to a simply materialistic modernization is to develop. Without political institutions and mores that give individuals and groups some freedom of expression, it is questionable whether the process of modernization can effect profound transformation in a society. Whatever else modernization may be, its ultimate objective is to bring about both material advancement and opportunities for the self-realization of the individual. The latter not only provides the moral justification for the new political and social order, but is, to a large extent, the mainspring of its material success.

To date, few Arab political systems have adopted reformist ideologies or their institutional concomitants, political party organizations, as the means by which to effect social and political change without destroying the fabric of societal and human relationships. For the greater part of its post-independence history, Tunisia has articulated a reformist ideology which has been committed to rational and scientific as well as humanistic resolution of the developmental dilemma confronting contemporary Arab man.

The dominant influence in the formation of Tunisian political values has been the Destourian Socialist Party under the ideological direction of the *ra'is* or chieftain, Habib Bourguiba.

Of the varied components constituting the PSD's political belief system, three elements deserve special attention inasmuch as they have direct bearing on the nature and direction of the modernization process. These elements are the party's interpretations of man, nation, and society and the interrelationship of these three in the context of developmental change.

MAN: HUMANISTIC LIBERALISM

The ethical world view of Bourguibist ideology can be described, in the words of the *ra'is* himself, as "humanistic liberalism," meaning principally a preoccupation and overwhelming concern with the "promotion of man." The Tunisian leader regards this as the "supreme end and fundamental value" of all political action. An "authentic democracy," Bourguiba has argued, cannot be achieved unless there is a belief in human dignity and perfectibility which, in combination, can guarantee the "triumph of good sense and reason" over ignorance and demagoguery. This confidence in the "supreme power of reason" is an appeal to social harmony involving a sense of collective mission in behalf of man, state, and society. Elevating the individual's intellectual and material level should be the ultimate goal of all collective effort. As Bourguiba has indicated: "For us, the dignity of man is at stake. We think man is perfectible, and we refuse to believe that there are men who are irremediably bad. We first of all give them the benefit of the doubt, and we make the necessary effort of persuasion in order to strengthen our ranks."

Other components of this humanistic liberalism include, at the individual level, loyalty, honesty, candor, liberty, patriotism, work, and responsibility and, at the social level, justice, equality, fraternity, solidarity, and charity.

The relationship of man and modernization is an intimate

one for Bourguiba, for as he has indicated the objective is to make "a good citizen, capable of initiative, eager to learn and cooperate [so] that the battle against underdevelopment will be won." Humanistic liberalism does not merely acknowledge or tangentially incorporate the individual in the developmental process but regards him as the dynamic life-force which makes progress at all possible. Hence the need for a "psychological revolution" which will transform man and in the process restructure social and human relationships in a way that will make modernity possible.

Not unlike French radical thought of the Third Republic, Bourguiba believes in man's perfectibility "if his reason can be freed from the dead weight of tradition." According to Bourguiba's "message," given man's basically rational as well as social character, he can very well be molded into a good citizen with modern views, once he has been shown that both common interest and his own interests are interrelated. At this stage a general consensus can be reached concerning the government's goals and its methods, and a "true" democracy then becomes possible.

Humanistic liberalism is the vision of a modern open society that respects both individual liberties and social justice. It adheres to a liberal approach towards politics, one which assumes it to be a matter of trial and error, and regards political systems as pragmatic contrivances of human ingenuity and spontaneity.

Inevitably, however, it has not always managed to sustain its liberal ethic. In fact, the realization that the humanistic liberalism of democratic France, which was so assiduously inculcated in the educational experiences of Bourguiba's generation of gallicized elites, was not always appropriate to the sociopolitical exigencies of emerging nation-states unavoidably led to discrepancies between the European ideal and the Arab reality. This is particularly evident in the notion of "guided democracy" which constitutes an integral theme in reformist ideology.

In Tunisia democracy is defined in utilitarian and instrumental terms to the point that democratic liberties enjoyed by the citizenry are often merely a function of their congruence with the larger nationalist needs and objectives of the state as determined by the dominant elite. As long as the "battle against underdevelopment"—the populist theme often invoked by Destourian ideologues to rally the masses and suppress opposition—continues, individual liberties must correspond to the collective will of the state. As a result some of the progressive character of reformist ideology is dissipated by the heady insistence on individual conformity to the ideas and ideals of the ruling elite.

Inevitably, Bourguiba's stress on the unitary nature of Tunisian society serves to justify a monolithic political structure and the exercise of power on the basis of unanimity. This authoritarian streak in Destourian ideology is reminiscent of Rousseau's view of the organic character of the community and his identification of democracy with virtue, implying that autonomous intermediary groups, for example, could not insert themselves between the state and the individual.

Given the need to introduce, in as rapid a fashion as possible, systemwide socioeconomic and political changes which often involve major dislocations of existing structural and human relationships, it is not surprising that certain authoritarian behavior patterns would manifest themselves among the top elite of the PSD. On balance, however, reformist ideology, unlike its radical and reactionary counterparts, remains authentically humanistic with a moral commitment to liberal ideas of democracy and freedom, notwithstanding the occasional and partly explainable lapses into quasiauthoritarianism.

NATION: LOCAL NATIONALISM

Tunisia possesses distinct and historically identifiable national roots. While the country over the centuries has been conquered by foreign invaders, it nonetheless has retained its individualism and nationalistic imprint. With the possible exception of a vestigial regionalism which has persisted into the modern era and which, on occassion, has been the cause of internecine conflicts, Tunisia has confronted no insurmountable societal division, class cleavage, or cultural fragmentation. For the most part Tunisia remains a geographically, ethnically, religiously, and linguistically homogeneous nation-state. Even in the tide of Pan-Arabism that has swept the Middle East and North Africa since the rise of Nasser in the mid-1950s, the country continues to espouse a local over a regional nationalism, notwithstanding the intermittent externally directed and diplomatically couched speeches, statements, and proposals to the contrary.

Inasmuch as Tunisia puts a premium upon its own nationalism at the expense of any higher supranational allegiance, it is distinguishable from all other Arab states. This recognition and acceptance of local nationalism as the psychocultural core of nation-state behavior constitute the second basic component of reformist ideology.

TUNISIAN NATIONALISM

Unlike most of the Arab and African countries, Tunisia has a long and distinguished recorded history. It has a tradition of physical and social unity and, in fact, on the eve of French colonial invasion Tunisia boasted a legacy of geographic continuity, religious and linguistic homogeneity, and comparative social solidarity. In fact, when French occupation started in 1881, Tunisia had long been a unified country, possessing all the institutions of a viable society. It did not have to discover that it was a state.

Thus when the Neo-Destour emerged as a modernist nationalist force in the 1930's, it did not have to create a sense of Tunisian nationalist consciousness among the people but simply resurrected a strongly rooted and deeply felt sense of Tunisian nationhood. Moreover, Bourguiba's nationalist appeals were not simply contrived slogans invoked and disseminated for the purposes of buttressing surreptitious subnational or transnational aspirations. Nor were they intended simply as political ammunition directed against French colonial rule. Rather, the Neo-Destourian leadership shared a collective commitment to an autonomous, independent Tunisian state as a means to gratify strongly felt psychocultural needs as well as establish the necessary political infrastructure by which to modernize a fundamentally traditional and backward society.

Clearly the characteristic political myths and symbolic outputs found among almost all nationalist ideologies in the Third World were likewise present in the Tunisian case. Tunisian nationalism served to center authority on certain aspects of tradition, asserted the continuity of society, and linked the present with the past. By so doing, it asserted the immortality of the society. Unlike many other African and Arab nationalist ideologies, however, Tunisia's process of nationalist mythmaking bore concrete historical roots and empirically verifiable links with the past. Hence its rather easy institutionalization among Tunisia's mass public.

What was imported, however, and found difficult acceptance was the gallicized component added by Bourguiba to form the core of modern-day Tunisian nationalism. In Bourguibist doctrine Tunisian nationalism stemmed from the original soundness of Tunisian tradition fortified by interaction with and assimilation of French civilization.

From its inception the PSD, under Bourguiba's control, has helped to define Tunisia in both its Arab and Mediterranean components. Based on history and geography and given Bourguiba's pro-French orientation, it was not difficult to create a nationalist synthesis derived equally from both oriental and occidental sources. The rise of an aggressive Pan-

Arabist movement, however, gave urgent impetus to Bourguiba's particular brand of nationalism, especially in the wake of the strong pro-Arabist Youssefist movement of the late 1950s which had wide popular appeal among Tunisia's masses and was very close to overturning Bourguiba's reformist political system.

Determined to guarantee the nationalist configuration of an independent Tunisia free from the overt influences of transnationalist Arabic currents, Destourianism resurrected and subsequently reified the historical uniqueness of the Tunisian nationalist experience. "For thousands of years," Bourguiba stated in a 1964 speech at Le Kef, "Tunisia has played a part in the great currents of civilization. It is thus that in Carthage and Kairouan, Mahdia and Tunis, vast empires were born, characteristic in their great concentrations of people. Whether one originates from Tunis, the south or the Sahel, one can only react as a Tunisian, that is with a strong sense of belonging to the one and same family: the Tunisian nation."

The centrality of Tunisia in the Mediterranean world constitutes Bourguiba's historical rationalization of his country's cultural "duality"; hence the much-invoked "crossroads" theory of history. "Tunisia occupies a strategic position on the Mediterranean," Bourguiba asserted on the occasion of the second anniversary of the French evacuation of the naval base at Bizerte. "As attested to by history it is a crossroads, a confrontation point of rival civilizations intent on destroying each other."

The PSD leadership is conscious and proud of its Mediterranean heritage. "Cradled in the center of the Mediterranean basin," Bourguiba has written, "Tunisia has been, from the earliest times, affected by the great successive currents of civilizations. The Tunisian population is the product of consecutive waves of peoples in which the Arab influence is predominant, but where the impact of other Mediterranean peoples can definitely be felt particularly in Tunis. From the time of its first contact with French civilization Tunisian society has exhibited a strong disposition to become a modern Western nation."

While the notion of a Mediterranean heritage and the development of a Franco-Tunisian synthesis appeals to many of Tunisia's westernized elite, it seems uncertain to what extent the masses' essentially traditional, Islamic base fully accepts this elite-generated aspect of the nationalist ideology. Obviously, Tunisia's mass public gives more than grudging acknowledgment to Tunisia's Arabic and Islamic heritage in both its historical and contemporary dimensions. And even among many of the country's educated groups and non-governing elites there is increasing affinity with Islamic culture and tradition. In fact, the overwhelming majority are convinced Muslims in a liberal sense, with a strong emotional attachment to Islam, but they stress the cultural rather than the strictly religious heritage of which they are proudly conscious and from which they derive an intellectual indebtedness. In this aspect of the nationalist ideology many of the younger elites-to-be differ significantly from their elders-in power: the former are seeking to reaffirm the universal qualities of Islam rather than to ignore, suppress, or amalgamate them within a European-oriented cultural matrix. At heart the modernist intellectuals stand for a renewal of Arab-Muslim values and not for a radical break with the past.

In recent years the ruling nationalist elite, conscious of the declining popularity of Western-inspired images and symbols among an Islamic-oriented population, has sought to invoke traditional religious symbols as a means of buttressing its rule. Direct attacks as such bastions of Islamic fundamentalism as the Ramadan fast have long been discontinued, and the governing elite has now assumed a more positive or functional orientation towards Islamic practices and institutions.

For many, however, Bourguiba remains the "radical innovator" who has given an objective and practical meaning to the concept of *patrie*. The fatherland is defined by specific borders, where ancestors are buried, where today's generation toils, and where its children will be born. To the masses the appeals of fatherland are strong, as is Bourguiba's notion of an organic nationhood where the people are organized on the land they own, working together in pursuit of common goals, fated to a common destiny. In its very essence the Tunisian personality remains Arab and Muslim, and it is around and through this personality that the people must achieve unity.

For the most part the Bourguibist system has managed to successfully integrate the Arab-Muslim identity into a secular although not necessarily Western notion of Tunisian nationalism. Whatever else may happen to ideology and organization in post-Bourguiba Tunisia, a "sense" of secular nationalism with which all Tunisians identify, however much they may differ in its interpretation, seems certain to continue.

SOCIETY: DEVELOPMENTAL SOCIALISM

The ideas of nationalism, independence, economic development, and socialism are all intricately and subtly interwoven in new nations. Frequently with the successful completion of the preindependence struggle and the resolution of the national identity dilemma, indigenous elites turn toward the tasks of modernization and development often within a uniquely Third World socialist framework. As has often been observed, developmental socialism is a reorientation of nationalism to meet the challenge of independence.

The PSD subscribes to one form or another of developmental socialism which is different from classical Western socialism: neither orthodox Marxism nor classical socialist arguments, it is contended, apply directly to the conditions and cultures of Third World societies to which Tunisia is intricately bound. Moreover, developmental socialists believe that they have improved on the theoretical apparatus of socialism thereby making it more relevant to contemporary societal needs. Finally, developmental socialists assert that the distinctiveness of their approach to socialism is rooted in the historic cultures or the native philosophies of their people.

Unlike orthodox Western socialism, developmental socialism is largely silent on the subject of class antagonism and is often vague or ambiguous about the role of property. Since developmental socialists are essentially indifferent to property relations, they see little value in private enterprise that is productive and nonexploitative. Their socialism invariably envisages a mixed economy with the government, however, determining both degree and scope of the mixture.

The common element in developmental socialism in its various doctrinal nuances is the emphasis on developmental goals and modernization for which all individuals must make sacrifices. While developmental socialsm is not primarily a doctrine of governmental control of the economy, government is accepted as the main source of development. According to articulators and supporters of a socialist philosophy, the advantages of developmental socialism is that it offers unified developmental goals that stress roles functional to modernization and the achievement of a workmanlike, rational society in which people lend one another a helping hand because they feel themselves a part of the community effort toward industrialization.

DESTOURIAN SOCIALISM OR DESTOURIANISM

Destourian socialism is not unlike other forms of developmental socialism characteristic of Third World mobilizational systems. Destourianism would fall somewhere between "communitarian socialism," wherein socialism is identified with the vision of harmonious social order, of development achieved without the dehumanizing consequences of radical individualism, and "moderate reformist socialism," which uses governmental institutions to direct an essentially private and pluralistic economy and society toward developmental goals. The process of development is thus viewed as gradual and democratic, achieved without cataclysmic upheaval or coercive regimentation.

The thrust of Destourianism is its attempt to translate Bourguibist ethical concern with humanistic liberalism into a concrete developmental goal involving the rational use of human and natural resources, equitable distribution of wealth, industrial and agricultural growth, social justice, sectorial and regional development, and, until 1969, the emphasis on cooperatives as the highest form of economic and social organization. Its concept of property as social function and its obsessive concern with individual effort for collectivist ends does not imply, however, a Marxist or even neo-Marxist orientation with which Bourguiba is at fundamental odds.

Probably Destourianism's closest historical counterpart is Fabian socialism. The Fabians' philosophy was a determinist view of history based on economics, but they did not believe that history makes great leaps, but rather small, cumulative adjustments. Thus social changes result from the adaptation of people to new conditions, and the driving force in change is not necessarily the class struggle but man's general tendency to adapt to new demands. In bringing about change, one can appeal to man's rationality and moral conscience outside any narrow class context.

The Bourguibist vision of Fabianism stresses socialism's pragmatic and utilitarian rather than doctrinaire qualities. As Bourguiba himself has indicated:

> The Tunisian plan is socialist, if socialism means the formation of a society that works for the benefit of the

majority and is based on an economy whose interest is the respect of man, ensuring balanced development that responds to his needs and possibilities within the framework of justice and equality.

This particular theme was reiterated at the eighth PSD congress held at Monastir in October 1971, where in his opening speech Bourguiba indicated:

In our eyes socialism is neither a philosophical belief nor an uncompromising social doctrine. It is not an end in itself. It is a means of achieving a precise objective, namely development. . . . By definition our socialism is distinguished from other socialisms by three fundamental aspects: (1) it rejects the class struggle; (2) government seeks to control and direct rather than eliminate private or collective property; finally, (3) we do not believe it necessary to sacrifice the present generation to guarantee the well-being of future ones. We remain firmly convinced of the need to pursue unswervingly our fight against underdevelopment.

According to the Destourian frame of reference national citizenship, representing unity, is the critical form of acceptance, with no other loyalties taking precedence over loyalty to the state. Behind unity is the concept of society as a natural, organic body, all parts of which have appointed functions, including the parts linked to the development process, which have the most significant functions.

For Bourguiba socialism does not mean class warfare; rather, the method of the party consists in rallying all together to attain socialist objectives. Moreover, state intervention is not an end in itself. It becomes necessary if the private sector proves inadequate, neglectful of the general interest, or badly managed.

Five years after independence it seemed that the liberal

economic policies hitherto pursued by Tunisia in its goal toward development had indeed been badly managed and required major alteration. This alteration took the direction of greater state control of land productivity and the form of a cooperative scheme under the leadership of former unionist Ahmad Ben Salah. This bold experiment in social engineering had the initial support and enthusiasm of Bourguiba who viewed it as an instrumental component of his utilitarian ideology.

It is noteworthy that in this transition from liberalism to socialism in 1961 Bourguiba retained the coherence and continuity of his original ideology with its human and nationalistic components. The dignity of man was reinterpreted to demand a greater effort at production and an insistence on better distribution of wealth in order to ensure material conditions for moral and intellectual growth.

Destourianism was being introduced as a pragmatic response to the needs of society reflecting Bourguiba's desire for efficiency and adaptability to new conditions. Theoretically, Destourian socialism retained its goal of transforming society through consent not coercion. The function of the state was simply one of coordinator, harmonizer, and regulator, for society itself should still generate its own decision-making centers so as to limit the powers of state control. In a 1965 Cairo speech Bourguiba outlined the relationship of state and individual under Destourianism.

> After having examined the results of the decision to adopt the Plan it appears that it was a step toward socialism, and that ineluctably, the evolution of economic and social structures would transform the means of production into a social property serving man.
>
> Our socialism does not *a priori* seek to destroy private property nor does the State practice a policy of outright nationalization. According to our beliefs the State substitutes itself for the individual in the pursuit of his well-

being only where it is better equipped to manage the individual's interests.

Yet the individual and his personal wants remain subordinate to the interests of the nation at large. And it is the function of the state to insure that the desired balance is achieved so as to guarantee justice and equality for all. "Destourian socialism is . . . opposed to the excesses of individualism, to blind selfishness," Bourguiba stated in a 1962 speech on planning. He continued:

> We then reasoned as follows: the old individualistic habits, systematic stand-offishness, in no way correspond to the urgent requirement of our recovery; collective efforts on the basis of solidarity between all of us as inhabitants of this corner of the earth, is the only solution for us. . . . The individual can no longer constitute a self-contained entity. He can no longer be regarded as an end in himself independent of his material and social environment. . . . The conception of society, the fact that we live together, must prevail.

The vulnerability of Third World Fabianism or moderate reformist socialism is its precarious resource base and small area of economic maneuverability which remain intimately tied to bourgeois interests and middle-class propensities. While Ben Salah may have overextended himself in an attempt to achieve rapid and complete social and economic restructuring of Tunisian society, he nevertheless was operating within the Bourguibist paradigm, with its stress on individual and personal sacrifice for the good of the state, redistributive justice, and leveling of overt discrepancies in wealth and status.

The latent bourgeois character of Destourianism revealed itself most emphatically when Bourguiba in September 1969, put an abrupt end to the cooperativist experiment and jailed its administrative head. Undoubtedly, impulsive planning rather than rational economic calculations resulted in much discontent among the rural masses who were being organized in the cooperative system and inevitably had a direct effect on production levels and overall economic outputs. However, it is equally clear that the revolutionary socialist character of the cooperative scheme had alienated a significant stratum of the landed commercial petty bourgeoisie—the "5,000 families," 3 percent of all farmers, who owned half of all arable land—who constituted the traditional bulk of PSD support. This, in conjunction with increased international pressures from Western capitalist interests who kept Tunisia afloat through assorted loan arrangements and general assistance programs, were sufficient catalysts to dismember this socialist experiment and make a mockery of Destourian socialism. "At least twice Tunisia yielded to international presure," noted a Western-trained Tunisian social scientist: "once by introducing a stabilization program and devaluating its currency, and a second time, by promising the World Bank that it would not extend land reform beyond the north of the country." (Hermassi, 1972:191]

While the regime's experiment with production and marketing cooperatives in an effort to marshal resources, modernize traditional structures, absorb unemployment, and in general transcend the bifurcation between modern and traditional agriculture ended in failure, the PSD remains committed to the goals of developmental socialism notwithstanding the return of laissez faire in many sectors of the economy. By the mid-1970s, communitarian socialism had given way to moderate reform socialism where development was now seen as gradual and democratically controlled. With the increasing importance of foreign investment and the rise of national capitalistic interests, the government's role now appears to be one of regulating a predominantly private economy.

STRATEGY: BOURGUIBISM

The strategy and tactics employed by the ruling elite to translate the principles of Destourian socialism and humanistic liberalism into concrete policy have come to be known as Bourguibism. The hallmark of Bourguibism is its pragmatism as revealed in Bourguiba's *politique des étapes* or "step-by-step" diplomacy. This policy of stages involves the objective appraisal of forces and problems and the realistic setting of objectives. Moreover, this is a policy in which strategy is geared to the realization of what is attainable now, and yet currently contributes to the reach of long-range objectives.

The probable genesis of such an approach can be found in relationship with French colonial power and its control over Tunisia. Rather than a frontal assault on the colonial situation, Bourguibism had involved persuading the adversary that reforms leading to independence were in his best interest. Methods of persuasion rather than force were always preferred once it became obvious that violence used against the militarily superior colonialist would prove self-defeating and self-destructive to the viability of the Tunisian national independence movement. However, this did not preclude the use of force when the situation so required. "I have always been a firm believer in the use of force and political action sometimes concurrently in order to achieve a desired goal," Bourguiba once stated.

But the essence of Bourguibism, with the exception of the disastrous Bizerte conflict in 1961, has been its reliance on methods of persuasion, rationality, and mutual self-interest to achieve desired ends. "My method is to advance by steps, thinking out every step as I go. Speed does not mean hasty, unthought-out actions." Clearly this tactic proved most successful in achieving independence from France and, in the eyes of the masses at least, principal credit was given to

Bourguiba's step-by-step approach rather than to any actions undertaken by the French themselves in pursuit of their own national self-interest.

The legitimization of Bourguibism in the international arena was easily transferred into the domestic sphere. Now the adversary was defined as underdevelopment, illiteracy, economic backwardness, mismanagement and corruption, and crass self-seeking individualism. Not unlike its manifestation in foreign affairs, Bourguibism's internal objective was to modernize traditional Tunisian society within the framework of stable, evolutionary, and rational planning. The task of internal Tunisian development required gradual changes in attidudinal orientations and behavioral norms to be achieved through education, party, propaganda, and, most importantly, Bourguiba's oratory. The predominant role of pedagogy in the struggle to transform man and society is justified in the context of Destourianism's humanistic liberalism.

In the meantime, if revolutionary disruption of the structure of society is not to take place, a dedicated, competent and enlightened elite must assume leadership and control of the state. This enlightened elite, institutionalized in the PSD, works to elevate the individual to a stage of proper social consciousness wherein he would then be permitted to enjoy the full benefits of democracy and individual liberty. Until such time, however, the ruling group must work to guarantee the cohesiveness of all social and political action. Guided democracy is thus a critical component of Bourguibism if not its principal motivating force. Civic education and encadrement thus become the means by which to achieve good citizenship and, consequently, democracy. If neither works adequately then other forms of persuasion are invoked, including intimidation and discrimination. Ostensibly while no one is forced to accept the dictates of Bourguibism, aspirants to elite status have no other pathway short of violent opposition. In brief, the strategy known as Bourguibism is characterized by the following: *politique des étapes,* pedagogy, dialogue, and realism.

CONCLUSION

In the Arab world today what are the prospects for the institutionalization of a reformist over a radical or reactionary ideology? Internal developments in several Arab states during the early and mid-1970s seem to indicate a possible attenuation of extremist politics. Variations on a reformist theme, for example, apparently have taken hold in Egypt, Algeria, Sudan, and even Syria. Moreover, domestic policy processes appear increasingly to be influenced by a concern for the rights of the individual. In addition, public pronouncements reflect greater awareness of a nationalist as opposed to a supranationalist political identity. Finally, there are signs that incumbent elites of previously revolutionary coloration are drawing up and implementing programs that are socially progressive and economically liberal yet which remain within a socialist-communitarian framework. Radical rhetoric and capricious behavior thus seem to be giving way to rational planning and reasoned decision-making.

Paradoxically, it is in the most moderate and democratic of Arab states that reformist ideology seems to have experienced a kind of setback. In Tunisia, for example, the abrupt termination of the cooperative experiment and the imprisonment of Ahmad Ben Salah has compromised the socialist component of developmental socialism. Powerful conservative forces in the ruling elite who felt their most vital interests threatened were successful in getting Ben Salah dismissed from public office and charged with high treason.

Despite the return to a modified form of laissez-faire, inflation, and growing unemployment, the PSD and Tunisia continue a moderate program of economic and social development that puts great emphasis on private enterprise and private foreign investment.

Another indication of the apparent dilution of reformist ideology in Tunisia was revealed at the PSD's ninth party congress held at Monastir in mid-September 1974. At that time attempts at further liberalization of democratic principles both within the party and the nation-at-large proved unsuccessful. In fact, Bourguiba was proclaimed president for life thereby reestablishing his control over the country's political apparatus. The whole process of granting greater voice to rank-and-file party members by introducing elections at all party levels was likewise eliminated, although three years earlier at a similar congress in Monastir such a process was deemed essential for Tunisia's continued democratization.

And yet, through history, culture, national character, and the enduring exposure to the modern world, Tunisia and its people seem to have successfully internalized much of the humanistic and nationalistic components of reformist ideology, quite possibly permanently.

POLITICAL STRUCTURES AND INSTITUTIONS

Tunisia's major political institutions and structures—the PSD, cabinet, and the National Assembly—all bear the unmistakable imprint of President Bourguiba. As chief executive in a presidential regime, Bourguiba exercises great power. He is guardian of the constitution and has the authority to appointment his government, which is responsible directly to him, not the National Assembly or party. In general, he draws up the general policy of the country and controls its execution. The president is also designated as commander-in-chief of the armed forces and makes all military appointments. With the agreement of the National Assembly, which has always been forthcoming, the president also has the authority to ratify treaties, declare wars, and make peace. His initiative in legislation has priority over that of National Assembly members. He also ratifies legislation and has the power of veto, subject to a two-thirds overriding majority which has never been invoked since the postindependence constitution and assembly have been in place. Constitutionally, the president can convene special sessions of the parliament, may issue orders in council when the assembly is in recess—constitutionally limited to six months of the year—and may take exceptional measures in times of crisis. A constitutional amendment passed by the National Assembly on December 17, 1974, named Habib Bourguiba president-for-life.

In all his functions the president is assisted by a cabinet, headed by a premier, appointed by the president and responsible only to him. Since 1970 Hedi Nouira, a long-time Destourian and close friend of the president, has filled the premiership. In the event of death or incapacity of the president, the premier succeeds him until new presidential elections are held.

Bourguiba is also head of the PSD and its top decision-making body, the Political Bureau. Bourguiba's political domination is thus a consequence of his dual capacity as undisputed head of the undisputed ruling party, and as the president of the state and so the chief of its executive agencies. The party and the state hierarchies run parallel, with much interchange of personnel between them, and much mutual interplay. One exists in symbiosis with the other: both bureaucracies have overlapping staffs, vaguely differentiated functions, and parallel structures. Bourguiba, who takes advice from either or both as the feeling moves him, stands at the head of this "party-government." He has at his disposition both a hierarchical party organization for mobilizing the nation and a political cabinet for deciding policy. Yet there is no doubt that as the undisputed leader of his country Bourguiba does not allow independent or contradictory judgments to be made. There is no question, for example, that his cabinet members are assistants, advisers, and collaborators. As he indicated when he assumed the presidency in 1959: "Government policies are my policies; members of the cabinet are my secretaries of state, not independent ministers, and they will carry out my policies."

Along with his collaborators in the cabinet, Bourguiba's other policy-making body of approximately the same size, is the PSD's Political Bureau. There is much interaction between the two bodies and an overlapping although not duplicative membership. In both groups, however, the tendency has been toward centralization of power under Bourguiba's surveillance.

Legislative authority is constitutionally exercised by the people through the unicameral National Assembly which has 112 members directly elected to five-year terms at the same time as the presidential election. By eliminating all candidates on minority lists in favor of the majority list, the election rules deliver the assembly to the PSD alone. The party controls individual candidacies through its Political Bureau, which draws up the lists after consulting with the leaders of the national organizations.

The assembly must meet at least twice a year for sessions of no more than three months, but additional sessions may be called by the president or a majority of the assembly members. The president may dissolve the national assembly in response to a vote of censure against him and call for new elections, but if the newly elected assembly repeats the vote of censure, he must resign.

Since independence there have been four elections to the National Assembly: November 8, 1959; November 8, 1964;

November 2, 1969; and November 4, 1974. All have been won by PSD candidates. Since the demise of the Communist Party in December 1962, no organized political opposition has contested legislative elections which have been the exclusive domain of the ruling PSD. Understandably, therefore, the National Assembly has not commanded much respect or attention as a forum for serious political debate or where meaningful legislation originates.

The PSD National Congress, which meets at irregular intervals (five times since independence: 1959, 1964, 1971, 1974, and 1979), is the corresponding body in the party circles and commands slightly more attention since it elects the party's Central Committee and reviews government and party policies. Yet like the assembly and despite the apparent openness of the debates and procedures, the National Congress tends to follow the broad lines of Bourguiba's wishes.

In terms of local government Tunisia is divided into thirteen governorates or provinces. Each province is headed by a president-appointed governor, who is assisted by either appointed government council or elected municipal councils. The provinces are further subdivided into delegations, communes, and *cheikhats* (hamlets).

In general Tunisia's formal structures of party and government serve more to legitimate leaders and policies than to act as effective mechanism for interest aggregation or decision-making. Even the system's relatively stable constitutional apparatus and well-functioning electoral mechanism provide no guarantee that they will be institutionalized in the post-Bourguiba period. Indeed, the cult of personality that has long dominated Tunisian political life leaves uncertain the degree to which the "party-government" created by Bourguiba and his contemporaries will long endure his passing. As we have seen, Tunisian ideology seems committed to a democratic, pluralistic social-political order which the *ra'is* has encouraged, indeed initiated, but for which no autonomous or effective institutional structures yet exist. Those currently in place including the National Assembly, the PSD and its Political Bureau and National Congress, and the cabinet are all mere appendages to Bourguiba's system of personal rule with little capacity for independent action or influence. Given the relatively sophisticated level of political cognition and experience extant among many of society's educated elites both in and out of power, one should not be surprised, in the uncertain period following the president's demise, to see either a forceful rejuvination of democratic tendencies within existing political institutions, or their virtual elimination to be replaced by ones more representative of Tunisia's increasingly differentiated and pluralistic social order.

POLITICAL PROCESSES

Buttressing Tunisia's constitutional edifice and dominant political ideology has been Bourguiba's extensive tactical skills, employed effectively for over two decades, in establishing and maintaining the presidential monarchy. Assisting the leader have been two groups of ruling elites found in both party and government: the "old guard," long-time associates of the president who participated in the preindependence struggle and who gained their positions through long years of party service, and a second category of younger elites brought into government by Bourguiba himself because of their specialized education, technical skills, and modernist outlook. Yet neither group has been allowed to achieve an independent base of power strong enough to challenge the hegemony of Bourguiba's rule.

Not unlike the arbiter role being played in Morocco by King Hassan II, the Tunisian leader has retained his preeminent role in the political process by deftly manipulating and controlling his political subordinates. Indeed, the hallmarks of this system have been the Bourguibist techniques of cabinet shifts, displacement of leaders from sensitive to innocuous posts, and even changing the nomenclature from cabinet ministers to secretaries of state. Particularly effective has been the way dissidents have been removed from office, even forced into exile, but later rehabilitated and returned to positions of responsibility. Like his counterpart in Morocco, Bourguiba keeps his political lieutenants in a state of permanent insecurity as they struggle among themselves for presidential favor while never really knowing when their political stars may diminish or fall into eclipse or, in the extreme, be eliminated altogether, as occurred in the cases of Salah Ben Youssef and Ahmad Ben Salah.

As indicated earlier, it was probably Bourguiba's fierce struggle with Youssefism in the mid-1950s that convinced him of the unacceptability of allowing any of his associates in the PSD to gain an independent following or to express political ambitions of their own. This, combined with a limitless capacity for vanity and didacticism, led Bourguiba to purge and, less and less frequently, rehabilitate a succession of prominent personalities from their official positions. The most prominent recent example, of course, has been the case of Ahmad Ben Salah who was dismissed from his position as secretary general of UGTT in 1956, only to be brought back into government five years later as minister of planning. In 1969, however, after the disastrous failure of his cooperativist experiment, Ben Salah was once again removed from office, then tried for treason and jailed. Yet after his escape from prison in 1973 Bourguiba announced a general amnesty for political prisoners including Ben Salah and invited the latter to return home, thereby indirectly creating the possibility of reintegrating a former "deviant" into the official fold. Ahmed Tlili was similarly introduced to, then dismissed from, the leadership of the UGTT. Trade unionist Habib Achour was elected, dismissed, and disgraced, then again returned and later arrested and imprisoned. Mohamed Masmoudi was dropped from the PSD's political bureau in 1958 for allegedly encouraging the official party organ, *L'Action*, to make critical attacks on Bourguiba's personal rule, and on the lack of democratic guarantees, only to be readmitted less than four months later, dropped once more in 1961, appointed foreign minister in 1970, then, in the aftermath of the Tunisian-Libyan merger fiasco with which he was strongly identified, he was ousted in 1974 and expelled from the party in disgrace. Bahi Ladgham, at the zenith of his popular appeal in 1970 when he was appointed chairman of the committee to supervise the implementation of the Cairo agreement between King Hussein of Jordan and the Palestine Liberation Organization, was removed as prime minister less than a year later. After his unexpectedly popular showing in the Central Committee elections at the 1971 PSD national congress, Ladgham was completely purged from the party and, two years later in March 1973, he resigned from all his political posts in the government and party. Ahmed Mestiri, long associated with the party's so-called liberal wing, was dismissed from his cabinet position as minister of the interior and then the party in 1971 and 1972, respectively, when he demanded greater liberalization of the government. In May 1973, in a final *coup de grace*, Mestiri was ousted from the National Assembly. In 1974, six men, including four former ministers, were expelled from the party for being critical of Bourguiba's blatant manipulation of the 1974 party congress in Monastir.

This system of political musical chairs has long been a trademark of Bourguiba's style of running things. The Tunisian leader's ability to engineer these successive purges while maintaining his patrimonial authority over both the government and the PSD can be explained in part because of his own enormous prestige as the father of his nation, partly because of his deftly developed skills as a tactitioner—always eliminating his potential challengers one at a time while maintaining the support of others—and partly because of the continuing availability of extremely talented individuals who have managed the affairs of state and party in effective style.

The ensconcement of patrimonial leadership has been accomplished through the instrument of the PSD. As the ruling party in a strong single-party system, the PSD has come to represent political power itself. While broad and continuous consultation occurs at all levels, all important decisions within the party come from above and are transmitted downward through the party hierarchy. The lower branches of the hierarchy enjoy considerable latitude in expressing local grievances, provided they are not of such a nature as to embarrass, compromise, or threaten the regime; but policy is not discussed at branch level—it is explained and received.

At the top of this hierarchy, of course, stands Bourguiba. In fact, party discipline and loyalty to the *ra'is* are scarcely distinguishable. Unlike competitive party systems in the West, the PSD is organized less to articulate and aggregate interests or act as a mechanism for decision-making as much as to give substance to Destourianism and Bourguibism; in the final analysis the party's primary function is a pedagogical one, transmitting the president's messages to his people.

Yet even this function may be diminishing as the party's credibility as the representative of the people is repeatedly compromised under the authoritarian aegis of the leader. Bourguiba used the party to ensure national unity by reducing all dissident centers of power whether on the left (Ben Salah), right (Mestiri), or center (Ladgham). Likewise, this same process was played out in the other national organizations representing businessmen and artisans, farmers, youth, and students, all of whom became virtual adjuncts of the PSD's

Political Bureau which was firmly in the control of Bourguiba himself.

On October 2, 1958, the president inaugurated a major reform of the party structure, the principal purpose of which was to assure his hegemony over the party. At the regional level, for example, the party's previously democratically elected federations were supplanted by commissioners appointed by the Political Bureau. Bourguiba justified such a reform by citing the need for cohesion, discipline, and administrative efficiency in a developing polity.

This process of consolidation and centralization was also apparent in other sectors of party-government relations: certain high party officials were disciplined for "improper" interventions into governmental affairs; the upper levels of the party hierarchy were transformed into docile sounding boards for the government; the party's representative organs, such as the National Congress and the National Council, were hardly ever convened and, when they met, demonstrated little independence, meeting simply to express solidarity and approval; the Political Bureau itself, supposedly consituting the party's executive decision-making body, was reduced under the impact of presidential government to a ceremonial role and, like other party organs, limited to advisory functions; its one important element of strength lies in that sometimes Bourguiba requires its corporate consent to a policy in order to legitimize it in the eyes of the party faithful.

What Bourguiba had, in fact, accomplished was the excessive concentration of power into his own hands creating a veritable "popular monarchy" or "presidential monarchy." The party paid a heavy price for Bourguiba's authoritarianism—a mere four years after independence Tunisia's single party began to lose popularity among the people as reflected in the decline by half of paid party membership in the party's historic stronghold, the Sahel, and the increasing autonomist tendencies apparent among the party's students, workers, and youth. This pattern has progressed to near disastrous levels in the two decades since 1960, notwithstanding the brief flurries of party vitality and rejuvination in 1964 and 1971.

The most important role the party has historically played and continues to play today, however imperfectly and notwithstanding Bourguiba's aggrandizement of power, is that of legitimizing the Tunisian political system. It does this in symbolic and, to a lesser and lesser extent, substantive terms by providing a unifying national institution, a historical link with the recent preindependence past, a decision-making organ, and a forum for popular participation, however circumscribed.

The PSD's work is to some extent supplemented by the national organizations, the officially recognized professional bodies and interest groups which, however, lack an autonomous existence. Most of these groupings exist in part to facilitate communication from the government to interest groups, in part to represent professional interests. They are all strictly subordinated to the PSD, and none possesses sufficient strength of organization to play an independent role in the system. The only possible exceptions have been the union federation (UGTT) and student association *(Union Générale des Etudiants Tunisiens* or UGET).

Once considered the most autonomous and functionally specific trade union movement in the Maghrib, the UGTT has gradually been reduced to dependency status. Since 1965 it has played a subordinate role to the party and, like other institutional groupings in the state, its primary function is now limited to one of education and propaganda.

UGET was once an important instrument for the articulation of specific students interests and a valuable source for the recruitment of future party elites, as in the outstanding case of former UGET leader Mohamad Sayah who is currently secretary general of the party. Yet in both capacities the student association is no longer taken very seriously since its autonomy from the mid-1960s on has been virtually eliminated. Moreover, in the eyes of many students it has become a mere pawn of the party and a neglected appendage to Bourguiba's system of personalistic rule.

Successive attempts in the late 1960s and early 1970s by independent and leftist student forces to disengage UGET from the iron-clad control of the party proved unsuccessful further alienating greater numbers of students. Indeed, the almost yearly series of student demonstrations, strikes, and riots that have been directed against the regime since 1965, ranging from such mundane issues as poor cafeteria food to demands for the very overturn of the system, were clear evidence of UGET's spectacular decay. As a consequence, the organization has become unattractive both to enterprising students who are seeking an independent path but have no ambition to rise in the established order as well as to aspiring and incipient political elites.

Students probably constitute the regime's greatest single internal challenge. The system's increasing authoritarianism has disaffected many independent-minded university students who have responded with regular and intense demonstrations since the mid-1960s. Recent surveys of selected student populations representing a cross-section of ideological types seems to put into serious doubt the previously assumed effectiveness of the Bourguibist socialization process and the one-party structure in institutionalizing citizen support for the elite political culture, Destourianism, Bourguibism, and other components of the dominant ideology. Both attitude and behavioral studies seem to confirm the ineffectiveness of the socialization process, resulting not only in mass disaffection with specific leaders and policies but more fundamentally with the elite political culture itself and its ethical and ideological underpinnings. The overall result is that the system's future is not insured nor its ideology confirmed among Tunisia's elites-to-be.

The regime's response to student agitation has often been excessive as reflected in some of the severe prison sentences meted out to student leaders in the aftermath of university disturbances in 1967, 1968, 1972, 1974, 1976, and 1978. If anything, these actions have only catalyzed the support of previously apolitical or politically neutral students for leftist demonstrators and their causes despite Bourguiba's policy of granting amnesty for many of the imprisoned demonstration leaders. Even recent conciliatory gestures by the party, including offers to reconstitute UGET into a more independent organization, have been turned down by the popular leftist student association, the Provisional University Committee. Many other dissatisfied students and intellectuals are being grouped around the "social demorcrats" of the National Council for the Defense of Public Liberties, an umbrella organization lead by former PSD leader Hassib Ben Ammar representing a broad cross-section of anti-Destourian or, at least, antiauthoritarian sentiment.

Yet none of these developments signal an imminent threat to the regime even if one includes disgruntled elements of the traditional religious classes. The small yet effective army, in terms of internal defense, is loyal to the regime. Nonetheless, the legitimacy of the regime's leaders, institutions, and ideology may be seriously contested in the immediate post-Bourguiba period, thereby leaving in great doubt the wisdom and political efficacy of current authoritarian policies being pursued by president and party.

POLITICAL ECONOMY

Tunisia's political economy of development has passed through three distinct phases since independence. From 1956 to 1961, the government pursued a liberal economic, laissez faire policy. The results of private investment and initiative, however, were disappointing since the natural movement of these years was the exodus of the resources Tunisia most needed—capital and skill—as the French left. In 1957, for example, the investment rate decreased from 19.5 percent of 1953, to 7.7 percent. Despite a vigorous fiscal policy, the backing of the currency, the creation of national companies of import and export, and limited experiments in land modernization, the economic situation continued to worsen. By 1961 the liberal economic policies were scrapped. Bourguiba called upon a group of unionists and administrators who had long preached the adoption of planning led by Ahmad Ben Salah who was appointed secretary of state for planning and financing.

From 1961 to 1969, Ben Salah, who had the full support of Bourguiba and the government as a whole, was given the task of developing a planned economy, with strict economic control assuring a protected internal market as well as a fixed exchange rate and currency regulation. A ten-year developmental perspective (1962–1971) was then drawn up the objectives of which were to solidify, in humanitarian terms, the meaning of Destourian socialism, especially its developmental component whose goal was the welfare of man, for the benefit of all social classes in proportion to their efforts and also their needs. The first three-year (1962–1964) and four-year (1965–1968) plans had four broad objectives of economic and social development: (1) decolonization; (2) reform of economic structures, including industrialization; (3) human development, including education, the training of cadres, and the fight against illiteracy and unemployment; and (4) self-development, so that investment could come from internal resources and not be dependent on foreign assistance.

Some of the more specific objectives of Ben Salah's labor-oriented development plan included the attainment, by 1974, of a minimum income of $100 per capita for the most disadvantaged strata, to limit foreign aid to 50 percent of the new investment to be undertaken, and to attain a savings rate of 26 percent of the GNP by the final year 1971. To ensure achievement of these goals a 6 percent growth rate was calculated. Yet these objectives were totally unrealistic since they required a tremendous amount of investment—an amount that was, in fact, disproportionate to the real economic capability of the country.

The most distinctive feature of the Tunisian political economy in the 1960s was the promotion and imposition of a cooperative system in production and trade. It was intended that cooperatives should play an important political and social role in the development of the country. It was also expected that the system would provide the key to a range of economic problems and would bring about a far more efficient mobilization of the country's resources. Yet the socialist experiment was eventually discontinued mainly because of the disastrous failure of the agricultural cooperatives. This sudden reversal which occurred with the dramatic dismissal of Ben Salah from his post as minister of planning, reflected the inherent difficulties of a government torn between the affirmation of economic independence and the need to compensate for its lack of indigenous resources through foreign aid, and between the desire to win over the rural masses and its fear of alienating the landowners.

As previously discussed, influential capitalist forces abroad and at home, as well as Ben Salah's evident mismanagement of the agricultural sector, led to the complete dismantling of the socialist system and the reestablishment of a liberal economic policy which was put into effect by Prime Minister Hedi Nouira in the early 1970s. This is the third and most recent phase of Tunisian economic development.

Current government policy has stressed the need for

greater foreign private investment. An April 1972 law, for example, gave major fiscal advantages to foreign companies investing in production principally for export. This and subsequent liberal laws have virtually abdicated a portion of Tunisian sovereignty in the eager pursuit of foreign capital. Stressing the availability of cheap labor and the absence of social conflict, Tunisian authorities have voluntarily shifted Tunisia into the ranks of those Third World countries where development is carried out by, and for the benefit of, foreign investors. In fact, the 1972 law will provide Tunisia with very few benefits since there will be no government revenues, no significant training and development of management expertise since the law allows the free entry of alien staff, no creation of local sources of capital since profits are repatriated, and few employment opportunities for skilled or semiskilled workers since only jobs for unskilled labor will be created, a category of people for which there is already an abundant supply. What will inevitably happen, of course, is that rather than emigrating, as some 15,000 Tunisians annually do, to become the proletariat of industrial Europe, the government is encouraging the bringing of foreign industry to these unemployed Tunisians, who will thus become an indigenous proletariat, while the profits flow out of the country unchecked.

In the short run at least, the overall shift in economic policy has proved beneficial. The redress of the economic and financial situations, and the attempt by Nouira's government to create an environment of trust and reconciliation, enabled the country, in 1971, to attain a rate of growth slightly above 7 percent. Despite the fact, however, that a greater degree of rationality in economic management has been introduced and the long-term prospects for economic growth seem bright, Tunisia continues to face several difficult economic conditions; namely, substantial unemployment, a massive balance-of-payments deficit, and an increasing foreign debt burden.

FOREIGN POLICY

Tunisian foreign policy is the product of one man: Habib Bourguiba, whose views on foreign affairs have been greatly influenced by his "French connection." He has consistently taken a moderate, pro-Western position on international issues going to the extreme of being virtually the only Third World leader to have given consistent support to American policy in Vietnam.

As a product of Western liberal thinking and aspiration, Bourguiba has shunned radical and extremist politics. For this reason he has fundamentally distrusted the communist bloc, especially Maoist China, and has been suspicious of those Afro-Arab leaders who have sought communist friendship in the form of military aid agreements and/or tacit military-political alliances. Given the country's basic goals in foreign policy of maintaining its independence and developing its resource-poor economy, it was only natural that Tunisia would turn to the United States as a countervailing force to communist power. As a result the United States has become Tunisia's principal supplier of economic assistance, both private and governmental. In fact, in the early 1960s per capita nonmilitary aid to Tunisia was greater than that given to any other developing country.

Tunisia continues to show a close affinity with France with whom it maintains extensive cultural, educational, and commercial ties. While the United States is regarded as the world's preeminent economic and military power, Bourguiba and his generation of gallicized elite consider France the most influential cultural, intellectual, and "spiritual" force.

Thus the Bourguibist approach has been to cultivate close ties with a United States which could provide a guaranteed protection to Tunisia while financially underwriting the country's extensive developmental efforts and, at the same time, remaining within the French cultural orbit. To date these objectives have been achieved, to one extent or another, via a policy of moderation, pragmatism, and a sense of proportion. Yet with all this, Tunisia has not compromised its nonaligned status as it continues to maintain proper diplomatic and economic relations with all the major states of the communist world and the "revolutionary" powers of the Third World.

Ironically, its pro-Western orientation has brought Tunisia into conflict with her own Maghribi neighbors, Algeria and Libya. The failure to implement the hastily announced Tunisia-Libyan merger in January 1974, led to mutual recriminations and accusations of political subversion and military conspiracy. Like its tense yet proper relationship with Algeria, Tunisia stands out in sharp ideological contrast with the puritanical, fundamentalist, and fervently Arabist Libya of Colonel Qaddafi. Given the profound differences in style, temperament, and political orientations, it can be expected that underlying tensions and occasional verbal if not military outbursts will most likely continue to characterize Tunisia's relations with Libya and, to a lesser extent, Algeria.

In the Middle East Tunisia has remained purposively aloof, giving verbal support to the Palestinian cause yet offering to mediate a permanent Arab-Israeli settlement based on a negotiated rather than military solution. On this issue, however, the Bourguibist elite are seriously estranged from the attitudes of students and workers who advocate a much closer affinity with Palestinian aspirations including more direct Tunisian participation in the struggle against Zionism.

A significant develop in this regard may have occurred with the transfer of the Arab League headquarters from Cairo to Tunis in 1979 in reaction to Egypt's peace treaty with Israel. Besides creating an important new outlet for employment of Tunisian elites and highly educated manpower, it will also draw Tunisia more closely into the Arab world sphere of influence with its concomitant impact on cultural ties and geopolitical orientation of the Tunisian elite.

For the most part Tunisia's moderation in foreign affairs and consistently pro-Western orientation has been well rewarded by extensive American and other Western economic aid, assistance that has become essential to the country's internal development. Yet with all this Tunisia's credibility as a nonaligned Third World state has not been compromised as its relations with both the Soviet Union and China demonstrate.

In conclusion, Tunisian foreign policy goals have been modest, its techniques eminently practical and realistic, and its results undramatic yet proportionately rewarding. Given the country's small size, limited resources, and military vulnerability, Bourguiba has managed to establish a respectable position for Tunisia in world affairs. This even more than his considerable accomplishments within the domestic sphere will probably be Bourguiba's most lasting legacy.

BIBLIOGRAPHY

For historical reasons research and writing on the three North African states of Algeria, Morocco, and Tunisia have been dominated by French scholarship and French-language literature. In recent years, however, more and more first-rate publications on the Maghrib have appeared in English to such a degree that students can now adequately resort to the English-language literature for an introductory understanding of North African society and politics. This select book bibliography concentrates exclusively on English-language materials of either original works or translations. For the beginning student with little or no French-language competence this bibliography will be more than sufficient for his needs. In addition, many useful bibliographical citations may be found in the books listed below as in the Zartman reader, which includes a comprehensive annotated bibliography of English- and French-language materials.

GENERAL

The history of the preindependence period with concentrations on precolonial and colonial North Africa are well provided for in Jamil M. Abun-Nasr, *A History of the Maghrib* (Cambridge: Cambridge University Press, 1975); Charles-André Julien, *History of North Africa—Tunisia, Algeria, and Morocco: From the Arab Conquest to 1830* (New York: Praeger, 1970);

and Abdallah Laroui, *The History of the Maghrib: An Interpretative Essay* (Princton, N.J.: Princeton University Press, 1977), the latter two being English translations of original French works. The colonial Maghrib and the period of the national independence struggles involving both general as well as country-specific analyses can be found in: Jacques Berque, *French North Africa: The Maghrib Between Two World Wars* (London: Faber and Faber, 1967); John K. Cooley, *Baal, Christ and Mohamed: Religion and Revolution in North Africa* (New York: Holt, Rinehart and Winston, 1965); Alal al-Fassi, *The Independence Movements in Arab North Africa* (New York: Octagon Books, 1970); Charles F. Gallagher, *The United States and North Africa: Morocco, Algeria, and Tunisia* (Cambridge, Mass.: Harvard University Press, 1963); David C. Gordon, *North Africa's French Legacy, 1954–1962* (Cambridge, Mass.: Harvard University Press, 1964); and Lorna Hahn, *North Africa: Nationalism to Nationhood* (Washington, D.C.: Public Affairs Press, 1960).

Studies devoted to comparative analyses of the three North African political systems include: Richard M. Brace, *Morocco, Algeria, Tunisia* (Englewood Cliffs, N.J.: Prentice-Hall, 1964); Manfred Halpern, *The Politics of Social Change in the Middle East and North Africa* (Princeton, N.J.: Princeton University Press, 1963); Elbaki Hermassi, *Leadership and National Development in North Africa: A Comparative Study* (Berkeley, Calif.: University of California Press, 1972); Malcolm H. Kerr, "Political and Economic Trends in North Africa," in A. L. Udovitch, ed., *The Middle East: Oil, Conflict and Hope* (Lexington, Mass.: Lexington Books, 1976); Clement Henry Moore, *Politics in North Africa: Algeria, Morocco, and Tunisia* (Boston: Little, Brown, 1970); and I. William Zartman, *Government and Politics in Northern Africa* (New York: Praeger, 1963). Samir Amin, *The Maghrib in the Modern World: Algeria, Tunisia, Morocco* (Baltimore: Penguin, 1970) is explicitly leftist in orientation with a focus on the political economy of North African development. Sizable portions of Michael C. Hudson, *Arab Politics: The Search for Legitimacy* (New Haven, Conn.:

Yale University Press, 1977), and James A. Bill and Carl Leiden, *Politics in the Middle East* (Boston: Little, Brown, 1979) deal with the North African political systems in a comparative way. Diverse social, economic, political, and anthropological themes are treated in several excellent anthologies and edited books on North Africa: Leon Carl Brown, ed., *State and Society in Independence North Africa* (Washington, D.C.: The Middle East Institute, 1966); Michael Brett, ed., *Northern Africa: Islam and Modernization* (London: Frank Cass, 1973); Ernest Gellner and Charles Micaud, eds., *Arabs and Berbers: From Tribe to Nation in North Africa* (Lexington, Mass.: Lexington Books, 1972); Ernest Gellner and John Waterbury, eds., *Patrons and Clients in Mediterranean Societies* (London: Duckworth, 1977); and I. William Zartman, ed., *Man, State and Society in the Contemporary Maghrib* (New York: Praeger, 1973).

Two reference works in English are particularly useful to the introductory student. They are Wilfrid Knapp, *North West Africa: A Political and Economic Survey* (London: Oxford University Press, 1977); and *The Middle East and North Africa, 1978–79* (London: Europa, 1978).

The international politics of North Africa has yet to receive adequate book-length treatment in English. First-rate selective surveys may be found in A. L. Udovitch, ed., *The Middle East: Oil, Conflict and Hope* (Lexington, Mass.: Lexington Books, 1976); John Waterbury and Ragaei El Mallakh, *The Middle East in the Coming Decade: From Wellhead to Well-Being?* (New York: McGraw-Hill, 1978); John Waterbury, "The Soviet Union and North Africa," in Ivo J. Lederer and Wayne S. Vucinich, eds., *The Soviet Union and the Middle East: The Post-World War II Era* (Stanford, Calif.: Hoover Institution Press, 1974); Charles F. Gallagher, *The United States and North Africa* (Cambridge, Mass.: Harvard University Press, 1963); Clement Henry Moore, *Politics in North Africa* (Boston: Little,

Brown, 1970); and I. William Zartman, *Government and Politics in Northern Africa* (New York: Praeger, 1963).

The leading English-language scholarly journals treating the Maghrib on a regular basis are the *Middle East Journal, The Maghreb Review*, and the *International Journal of Middle East Studies*.

ALGERIA

Probably the single most comprehensive analysis of the complexities and dynamics of the Algerian revolutionary war fought against France from 1954 to 1962 is that of Alistair Horne, *A Savage War of Peace: Algeria, 1954–1962* (New York: Penguin, 1979). Paul Henissart, *Wolves in the City* (London: Rupert Hart-Davis, 1971) is a fascinating and chilling account of the last destructive, anarchic days of French colonial rule in Algeria. Martha Crenshaw Hutchinson, *Revolutionary Terrorism: The FLN in Algeria, 1954–1962* (Stanford, Calif.: Hoover Institution Press, 1978) formulates an analytical model of terrorism which she then applies to the case of the wartime FLN. More standard accounts of that bloody struggle for independence include: Edward Behr, *The Algerian Problem* (London: Hodder and Stoughton, 1961); Michael K. Clark, *Algeria in Turmoil* (New York: Grosset and Dunlap, 1960); Richard M. and Joan Brace, *Algerian Voices* (Princeton, N.J.: Van Nostrand, 1965); Richard M. and Joan Brace, *Ordeal in Algeria* (New York: Van Nostrand, 1960); Joan Gillespie, *Algeria* (New York: Praeger, 1960); David Gordon, *The Passing of French Algeria* (New York: Oxford University Press, 1966); and Alf Andrew Heggoy, *Insurgency and Counterinsurgency in Algeria* (Bloomington, Ind.: Indiana University Press, 1972). Brief analyses of the Algerian revolution are included in: Eric R. Wolf, *Peasant Wars of the Twentieth Century* (New York: Harper and Row, 1969), and John Dunn, *Modern Revolutions* (Cambridge: Cambridge University Press, 1972). Frantz Fanon, *The Wretched of the Earth* (New York: Grove Press, 1963), and Frantz Fanon, *A*

Dying Colonialism (New York: Grove Press, 1967) provide philosophical and highly ideological insights into the origins, causes, and consequences of the revolutionary war and its impact on native and colonialist alike. Fanon's credo on the need for the violent transformation of man, state, and society remains a central theme in the writings of many Third World revolutionary leaders. The impact of the Algerian war on French society and politics is competently treated by Tony Smith, *The French Stake in Algeria, 1945–1962* (Ithaca, N.Y.: Cornell University Press, 1978).

Pierre Bourdieu, *The Algerians* (Boston: Beacon Press, 1962) is outstanding in providing a socioanthropological insight into the colonialist system and the destructive effect it had on Algerian man and society. Thomas L. Blair, *The Land To Those Who Work It: Algeria's Experiment in Workers' Management* (Garden City, N.Y.: Anchor Books-Doubleday, 1970); Ian Clegg, *Workers' Self-Management in Algeria* (New York: Monthly Review Press, 1971); and Marnia Lazreg, *The Emergence of Classes in Algeria: Colonialism and Socio-Political Change* (Boulder, Colo.: Westview Press, 1976) focus in on specific socioeconomic themes and issue areas, while Sid-Ahmed Baghli, *Aspects of Cultural Policy in Algeria* (Paris: UNESCO, 1977) devotes his study to cultural policy in the Boumediene period.

Although over a decade old William B. Quandt, *Revolution and Political Leadership: Algeria, 1954–1968* (Cambridge, Mass.: The M.I.T. Press, 1969) remains the most authoritative study of Algerian political development at the elite level. The critical roles being played by military and other elites in independent Algeria are comprehensively analyzed by: I. William Zartman, "The Algerian Army in Politics," in Claude E. Welch, Jr., ed., *Soldier and State in Africa* (Evanston, Ill.: Northwestern University Press, 1970), and I. William Zartman, "Algeria: A Post-Revolutionary Elite," in Frank Tachau, ed., *Political Elites and Political Development in the Middle East* (New York: Schenkman, 1975). David and Marina Ottaway, *Algeria: The Politics of a Socialist Revolution* (Berkeley, Calif.: University of California Press, 1970), and Jean Leca, "Algerian Socialism: Nationalism, Industrialization, and State-Building," in Helen Desfosses and Jacques Levesque, eds., *Socialism in the Third World* (New York: Praeger, 1975) describe and evaluate Algeria's socialist experiment. Arslan Humbaraci, *Algeria: A Revolution that Failed—A Political History since 1954* (New York: Praeger, 1966) provides an informative although at times biased general political history of the country since the early 1950s.

Along with Knapp cited above the best reference work on Algeria is the *Area Handbook for Algeria* (Washington, D.C.: USGPO, 1979). The full range of Algerian society and politics are treated in the general comparative studies and edited books cited above.

MOROCCO

The history of preindependence Morocco including the precolonial, colonial, and nationalist phases is systematically analyzed by Douglas E. Ashford, *Perspectives of a Moroccan Nationalist* (Totowa, N.J.: The Bedminster Press, 1964); Stephane Bernard, *The Franco-Moroccan Conflict, 1943–1956* (New Haven, Conn.: Yale University Press, 1968); Robin Bidwell, *Morocco Under Colonial Rule: French Administration of Tribal Areas, 1912–1956* (London: Frank Cass, 1973); Edmund Burke, *Prelude to Protectorate in Morocco: Precolonial Protest and Resistance, 1860–1912* (Chicago: University of Chicago Press, 1976); and John P. Halstead, *Rebirth of a Nation: The Origins and Rise of Moroccan Nationalism, 1912–1944* (Cambridge, Mass.: Harvard University Press, 1967).

Islam's importance in Moroccan political and social life receives exceptional scholarly treatment by: Clifford Geertz, *Islam Observed: Religious Development in Morocco and Indonesia* (New Haven, Conn.: University Press, 1968); Dale F. Eickelman, *Moroccan Islam: Tradition and Society in a Pilgrimage Center* (Austin, Tex.: University of Texas Press, 1976); and Ernest Gellner, *Saints of the Atlas* (Chicago: University of Chicago Press, 1969).

A number of important sociological and anthropological themes in Moroccan life are conscientiously treated by: Kenneth

Brown, *People of Salé* (Cambridge, Mass.: Harvard University Press, 1976); Daisy Hilse Dwyer, *Image and Self-Image: Male and Female in Morocco* (New York: Columbia University Press, 1978); Vanessa Maher, *Women and Property in Morocco: Their Changing Relation to the Process of Social Stratification in the Middle Atlas* (London: Cambridge University Press, 1974); Paul Rabinow, *Symbolic Domination: Cultural Form and Historical Change in Morocco* (Chicago: University of Chicago Press, 1975); and John Waterbury, *North for the Trade: The Life and Times of a Berber Merchant* (Berkeley, Calif.: University of California Press, 1972).

The most reliable analyses of Moroccan political development and institution-building are: Douglas E. Ashford, *Political Change in Morocco* (Princeton, N.J.: Princeton University Press, 1961); I. William Zartman, *Morocco: Problems of New Power* (New York: Atherton Press, 1964); I. William Zartman, *Destiny of a Dynasty: The Search for Institutions in Morocco's Developing Society* (Columbia, S.C.: University of South Carolina Press, 1964); and John Waterbury, *The Commander of the Faithful: The Moroccan Political Elite—A Study in Segmented Politics* (New York: Columbia University Press, 1970), with the latter probably being the best work in any language on the nature of elite politics in Morocco.

Local government, public administration, planning, and aspects of economic development are the concern of: Douglas E. Ashford, *Morocco-Tunisia: Politics and Planning* (Syracuse, N.Y.: Syracuse University Press, 1965); Douglas E. Ashford, *National Development and Local Reform: Political Participation in Morocco, Tunisia, and Pakistan* (Princeton, N.J.: Princeton University Press, 1967); and John W. Behen, *The Economic Development of Morocco* (Baltimore: Johns Hopkins Press, 1966).

Rom Landau, *Hassan II: King of Morocco* (London: George Allen and Unwin, 1962), and Rom Landau, *Morocco Independent under Mohammed the Fifth* (London: George Allen and Unwin, 1961), are sympathetic accounts of King Hassan II and his father, Mohammed V. An English translation of Hassan's memoirs is now available in *The Challenge: The Memoirs of King Hassan II of Morocco* (London: Macmillan, 1978).

General surveys of Morocco include: Nevill Barbour, *Morocco* (New York: Walker, 1965); Lorna Hahn and Mark I. Cohen, *Morocco: Old Land, New Nation* (New York: Praeger, 1966); and Vincent Monteil, *Morocco* (New York: Viking, 1964).

Indispensable reference works include, from above, Knapp and the Europa publication as well as *Area Handbook for Morocco* (Washington, D.C.: USGPO, 1965).

Excellent specialized studies on Moroccan political, social, and economic life can be found in the anthologies and edited books of Zartman, Gellner and Micaud, and Gellner and Waterbury.

TUNISIA

Tunisia's colonialist experience is sensitively treated by a Jewish native-son, Albert Memmi, *The Colonizer and the Colonized* (Boston: Beacon Press, 1967). Several works deal with Tunisia's political history from the precolonial period through independence such as: Charles F. Gallagher, "Tunisia," in Gwendolen M. Carter, ed., *African One-Party States* (Ithaca, N.Y.: Cornell University Press, 1962); Wilfred Knapp, *Tunisia* (London: Thames and Hudson, 1970); Leon Laitman, *Tunisia Today: Crisis in North Africa* (New York: Citadel Press, 1954); Dwight L. Ling, *Tunisia: From Protectorate to Republic* (Bloomington, Ind.: Indiana University Press, 1967); and Nicola Ziadeh, *Origins of Nationalism in Tunisia* (Beirut: Khayat's, 1962).

As one of the few instances of evolutionary political development in the Third World, Tunisia has received its share of scholarly attention. Such themes as modernization, social change, and political development are all intelligently treated by: Douglas E. Ashford, *National Development and Local Reform: Political Participation in Morocco, Tunisia, and Pakistan* (Princeton, N.J.: Princeton University Press, 1967); Willard A. Beling, *Modernization and African Labor: A Tunisian Case Study* (New York: Praeger, 1965); L. Carl Brown, "The Tunisian Path to Modernization," in Menahem Milson, ed., *Society and Political Structure in the Arab World* (New York: Humanities Press, 1973); and Charles Micaud with Leon Carl Brown and Clement Henry Moore, *Tunisia: The Politics of Modernization* (New York: Praeger, 1964). James Allman's *Social Mobility, Education and Development in Tunisia* (Leiden: Brill, 1979), deals with the impact of educational reform and expansion on Tunisia's development and modernization since independence.

Prospects for political institutionalization with special reference to Tunisia's single-party system are the concern of: Clement Henry Moore, *Tunisia Since Independence: The Dynamics of One-Party Government* (Berkeley, Calif.: University of California Press, 1965); Clement H. Moore, "Tunisia: The Prospects for Institutionalization," in Samuel P. Huntington and Clement H. Moore, eds., *Authoritarian Politics in Modern Society: The Dynamics of Established One-Party Systems* (New York: Basic Books, 1970); and Lars Rudebeck, *Party and People: A Study of Political Change in Tunisia* (New York: Praeger, 1969).

Sociological, cultural, and psychological studies of Tunisia can be found in Mark A. Tessler, "The Tunisians," in Mark A. Tessler, William M. O'Barr, and David H. Spain, eds., *Tradition and Identity in Changing Africa* (New York: Harper and Row, 1973); Russell Stone and John Simmons, eds., *Change in Tunisia: Essays in the Social Sciences* (Albany, N.Y.: SUNY Press, 1976); and Rafik Said, *Cultural Policy in Tunisia* (Paris: UNESCO, 1970).

Area Handbook for the Republic of Tunisia (Washington, D.C.: USGPO, 1979) provides adequate reference material for the country along with the Knapp book. Tunisia is given comprehensive coverage in the various general North African surveys identified above.

INDEX

COMPARATIVE POLITICS OF NORTH AFRICA

was composed in 11-point Linotype Times Roman and leaded two points
with display type in foundry Weiss Roman,
printed offset on 55-pound Glatfelter acid-free Offset Vellum,
by Joe Mann Associates, Inc.;
perfect-bound with 10-point Carolina covers
by Riverside Book Bindery, Inc.;
and published by
SYRACUSE UNIVERSITY PRESS
SYRACUSE, NEW YORK 13210